From SCOTLAND'S Past

by

Jenny Chaplin

FROM SCOTLAND'S PAST

CONTENTS

FROM SCOTLAND'S PAST

by Jenny Chaplin

ACKNOWLEDGEMENTS

1. D. C. Thomson & Co Ltd, publishers of "THE SCOTS MAGAZINE", the world's top-selling Scottish interest title, for their kind permission to include in this book the chapter entitled "The Blantyre Calamity".
2. Donald Currie, Editor of the long-established and world-renowned newspaper, THE BUTEMAN, for kind permission to quote from the antiquarian copies of THE ROTHESAY EXPRESS/ THE BUTEMAN and THE ROTHESAY CHRONICLE.
3. Ken Laird, publisher of SCOTTISH MEMORIES.
4. Angus J. Ray, Editor/publisher of THE HIGHLANDER, the magazine of Scottish Heritage, to the pages of which prestigious American magazine, the author is a frequent contributor.
5. Librarian Eddie Monaghan and his staff at Rothesay Public Library.
6. Kinnon Enterprises, publishers, Winnipeg, Canada.
7. Captain J. M. Chaplin M.N. (Ret'd).
8. John Murphy, an Honorary Vice-President and founding father of the 1820 Society.
9. Ian O. Bayne, Vice-Chairperson of the 1820 Society.
10. Iain R. McIntyre, Editorial director of BUSINESSLIKE Publishing.

INTRODUCTION

Most people, if they are being honest, will admit that they are fascinated by the various twists and turns of Fate which decide that one person becomes a plumber, another a poet, while yet another man or woman spends life as a doctor.

In studying the 'case histories' of many lesser-known Scots throughout the centuries, it is equally intriguing to find that in many instances what might be supposed to be the 'disadvantages' of very humble beginnings did nothing to deter the men and women featured in the following pages from making their mark in life.

Strangely enough, it was mainly the men -- "lads o' pregnant pairts", as one historian called them -- who rose from what were humble cottages, often little more than hovels; while the vast majority of women who achieved success, and again by their own efforts, came from the other end of the social scale -- the castles and mansions of Scotland which housed those high-born "Ladies of Quality".

All the characters featured in this book not only were well-known and highly respected in their day, but they gave help, pleasure and valuable service to their fellow-Scots, both in their own country and furth o' Scotland. The sad thing is that so very few of them are known today -- their talents, achievements and idiosyncrasies neglected and forgotten over the years.

Today, as we approach the end of the millennium, we often pause and congratulate ourselves on the 'progress' which has been made in so many fields -- not least of which are those of alternative and holistic medicine, new educational methods, positive thought, modern poetry, fanatical religious sects, women's liberation, and of course, 'sensible' eating and a multitude of dietary fads.

The amazing thing is that it has all been done before, and by these very self-same Scottish pioneers, whose achievements have lain neglected for far too long.

The purpose of this book is to remedy that situation so that those long neglected ghosts from the past may now take their rightful place in the pages of our country's history and at the same time, add their voice to Scotland's cultural heritage.

When I first started writing this book, I was well aware there would be no shortage of possible candidates for inclusion among the ranks of Scotsmen who were famous in their own day.

The very real difficulty, however, would lie in unearthing sufficient material relating to Scots-women. Most people, if they think about it at all, equate famous Scottish women with Carolina, Baroness Nairne, and the world-famed Flora MacDonald.

In fact, in my initial research, so thin on the ground appeared to be Scots-women of note from Scotland's past that my ever-helpful local Librarian, Eddie Monaghan, jokingly suggested a way out. The best thing might be for me to re-write that particular area of Scottish history ... and why not make a start with Florence MacNightingale!

That this somewhat revolutionary idea has not been necessary is thanks to Eddie Monaghan himself, the Librarian at Rothesay's Public Library, and his equally pleasant, generous and helpful staff. They helped me to dig deep into Scotland's cultural past -- and that without my even having to leave the 'Madeira of Scotland'.

From my summer-house writing 'den', far from telephones, surrounded by dozens of books, most of them borrowed on library "Project Tickets", and my desk overlooking "Sweet Rothesay Bay," I have been privileged to take not so much of a 'dauner' but rather more of a route-march down Scotland's Memory Lane. And in doing so I've been able to consider not just many unsung heroes and heroines of Scotland, but also many of the events and disasters which took place over the years, and which should not be allowed to disappear without trace into the mists of time.

Jenny Chaplin
Tigh na Mara Cottage
ROTHESAY
Isle of Bute
Scotland

ELSPITH BUCHAN (1738-91)

Scottish 'Saint' and Founder of the Buchanite Sect

For many years after the disbanding of the religious sect known as the Buchanites, probably their only claim to fame lay in the fact that for a time, no less a personage than Robert Burns was in love with a girl member of their group. Yet even he, romantic that he was, did not allow the rose-coloured spectacles of love to cloud his judgement as to who the Buchanites were and what they stood for. He went on record to describe these religious fanatics as 'carrying on a great farce by pretended devotion' and he stigmatized 'their idleness and indecency.' This latter comment may or may not have been influenced by the fact that although there were married couples within the group, by the strict rules laid down, they were not allowed to co-habit and 'all the responsibilities of the married state were given up.'

And what of their leader and instigator of the sect? What is known of her? How did she come to found the group? And what were their stated aims and ideals?

The first thing that must be said is that not only were the Buchanites well-known throughout Scotland in their day, but they had a tremendous impact - and not always for good - on several areas of the country. Indeed, so much notice had been taken of Elspith Buchan and her sect that her amazing religious zeal and equally astounding antics, gained her a place in the pages of 'The Biographical Dictionary of Eminent Scotsmen' (first published in 1832.) This singular honour was accorded to only a handful of other Scotswomen, such luminaries as Joanna Baillie, Lady Anne Barnard and the world-renowned and much-loved Baroness Nairne.

Later publications of various kinds also devoted much space to Elspith Buchan and her exploits, although it is perhaps worth noting that over the course of time, the spelling of her name changed to Elspeth. Whatever of that, she was born the daughter of an ordinary couple. Her father, John Simpson, an established businessman, kept an Inn situated between Banff and Portsoy. Born in 1738, as a child,

Elspith was brought up to the beliefs of the Scottish Episcopal Communion.

When once of an age to work and even at that tender age with a certain wanderlust, she was sent to Glasgow, where she entered service in the home of a well-to-do merchant who owned a pottery. Over the course of time, the young maidservant met and later married a man called Robert Buchan, who was a workman in the pottery belonging to her employer.

In her newly-married state, it appears that she lived happily enough with her husband and in the course of a few years, she bore him several children. Her husband's religious faith was that of a Burgher-Seceder, so Elspith thought it incumbent upon her to change her own beliefs and so join her husband in his. Having done so, she then tended to dwell rather too much on religious matters, to the point where, and no doubt to her husband's consternation, she got into the rather weird habit of interpreting the Scriptures literally.

She further began to "promulgate certain strange doctrines," which she derived in this manner from Holy Writ. This development obviously caused problems in the erstwhile happy home and in fact, hastened the end, and failure of her marriage. Next thing in the ongoing saga was that Elspith had left her husband and with two of her daughters, had decamped to Irvine, in Ayrshire. While there, she met and obviously highly impressed a Mr. Hugh Whyte, who was a Presbyterian Relief Clergyman. For some reason best known to himself, the said Reverend gentleman decided that not only was the recently arrived and now husbandless Elspith a Saint, she was also the embodiment of the woman mentioned in the Revelation of St. John the Divine (Chapter XII, verse 1.) which reads:

'And there appeared a great wonder in heaven; a woman clothed with the sun, and the moon under her feet, and.upon her head a crown of twelve stars.'

In this way, Hugh Whyte came completely under the spell of Elspith and together they formed the sect which was known as the Buchanites. And what was the immediate result of this action?

Amazingly, but perhaps on account of its novelty value, the newly-formed religious sect at first seemed to exert a weird fascination for the local community. So much so, that even the most unlikely and previously level-headed people hastened to join up with the Buchanites. Several 'trading people in good circumstances', a number of prominent local and upstanding citizens, and even a respected writer of the time, a Mr. Hunter, became converts with all possible speed.

And surprisingly enough, all went fairly smoothly for a number of years at Irvine. Then in April 1784, some unrecorded event and/or unacceptable act on behalf of the sect caused the local people to 'assemble in a threatening or tumultuous manner.' This they did around the environs of the Tabernacle of the new religion, a building which also served as Mr. Whyte's house. There were angry scenes, harsh words were spoken and a hail of stones, and other missiles were thrown at the windows, all of which were left broken before the night's work was done.

Events which followed on from this demonstration of anger and pent-up emotion, against the Buchanites and all they stood for, are somewhat of a grey area. Some historical reports have it that Hugh Whyte 'abdicated his charge', while others, not quite so polite, put it that he was 'ejected from his Ministry and exiled from Irvine.' Whatever the real version of subsequent events, the end result was the same - Elspith, the members of her sect, and Hugh Whyte, her Chief Apostle, were most certainly run out of Irvine by its hostile residents and equally outraged authorities.

The sum total of forty-six Buchanites left Irvine with all possible speed and set off, they knew not where. However, despite their previous trials, they still had unswerving faith in their 'spiritual mother' and her devoted Chief Apostle. So, without demur, they followed meekly in Elspith's wake. It is recorded for posterity that they proceeded through Mauchline, Cumnock, Sanquhar and Thornhill and did not halt until they arrived, no doubt footsore and weary, at a farmhouse some two miles south of Thornhill and thirteen miles from Dumfries.

One is tempted to speculate if it was in the course of this route march that Rabbie, ever alert to the charms of a pretty face, first caught sight of the new love in his life. Alas! Despite exhaustive research, that is one particular mystery the answer to which is lost in the mists of Time.

Anyway, safely arrived at the fairly remote farmhouse, the leader of the sect negotiated the hire of the outhouses as their living quarters and as the site of their proposed new Tabernacle. Their avowed hope was that in that lonely place and far from the influence of the outside world, they would be permitted to 'exercise their religion without further molestation.'

The commune lived happily enough and over time, amassed considerable wealth and property. Quite apart from the Law of non-cohabitation, 'Saint' Elspith kept adding new and even more strict rules and conditions of service for her Buchanites. Despite this, however, several of the tradesmen among them were given special dispensation by their 'spiritual Mother' which enabled them to work at their trades outwith the confines of the commune. It is interesting to note that this outwork they did gratuitously, and no doubt with the object of trying to spread their eccentric views and thus win over new converts.

Aside from this partial contact with the outside world, 'they abjured all worldly considerations, wishing only to lead a holy and quiet life till the Millenium, or the Day of Judgement,' which they believed to be at hand. And despite their leader's professed gift of prophecy and her 'ability to confer the Holy Ghost by breathing', she was nonetheless unable - and that in spite of her best efforts - to predict an exact date for their promised mass ascent to Heaven. Even so, and notwithstanding what many suspected as a sleight of hand with regard to some financial matters, there was, as yet, little sign of any dissatisfaction within the ranks. And except from those times of 'occasional rudeness of unbelieving neighbours', the 'little Republic lived in peace and happiness.'

But trouble was at hand. After a few false starts when the promised ascent to Heaven still did not materialise, there began to be a muttering and a gradual disillusionment spreading like a cancer through the religious community. This was especially so when the 'Saint' ordered her followers to cast aside all such vanities as rings, ornaments and anything else of value which they still possessed. The supposed idea behind this latest directive was to make their bodies that bit lighter for the onward, and hopefully, upward flight. When yet again nothing happened, Elspith blamed the failure on the twin causes of lack of Faith and the fact their bodies were still not yet sufficiently light.

'The 'Spiritual Mother' then came up with the bright idea of forty days and forty nights of Fasting.

As might be expected with her overweight and obviously over-indulged followers, this injunction did not go down at all well. Even worse, the commune members began to think that they would all die of starvation, thus leaving the non-fasting but still overweight 'Spiritual Mother' in sole possession of the cache of rings, brooches, ornaments, not to mention the very considerable monetary reserves of the Sect.

so increased the rigour of Elspith's discipline

And as had happened before, at the first sign of growing dissatisfaction, so increased the rigour of Elspith's discipline which must be obeyed by her followers. Obviously well tuned-in to the dark mutterings among the lower echelons, she decreed that there would, of necessity, be a new rule - anyone even suspected of considering leaving the Buchanite world would forthwith be locked up. Further to that, they would be released daily for the sole purpose of being ducked repeatedly in cold water.

In this way did Elspith manage to cling on to her somewhat disgruntled troops in her own religious army. Even so, and in spite of the very real dangers involved in trying to escape her clutches, in 1786 some brave souls did finally manage to secede.

On return to the real world in the West, they reported that apart from all other privations, Elspith kept the store and distribution of food provisions in her own domain, with the avowed and oft-repeated intention that they 'should not pamper their bodies with too much food.'

Left with a much-diminished band of disgruntled 'devotees', Elspith tightened the reins of command even further. And the strange thing was that while this fanatical régime was still under way, her abandoned husband, together with one remaining son, was still a faithful adherent of the Burgher-Seceders and still living out an ordinary life and going about his business in the usual way.

On her death bed in 1791, with her remaining strength, she called her Disciples together and with the help of her ever-faithful Chief Apostle, exhorted them to keep steadfast to her doctrine.

In desperation now to ensure the ongoing nature of the Buchanites, Elspith managed to gasp out that she had one last secret to impart - she really was the Virgin Mary, Mother of our Lord, and this despite her previous claims and counter-claims on this particular subject. Further to that, she begged them to believe that she was also that same woman mentioned in the Bible. Her version was that 'clothed with the sun' and driven into the Wilderness, she had been wandering in the world since our Saviour's day and only for some time past had she sojourned in Scotland. Thus, though to their eyes, she might appear really to die, in truth, she would but sleep a little and in a short time would return in her Glory, then to lead them to the New Jerusalem.

Persuasive to the last, with her dying breath she made her followers promise to await her Third Coming . She got her message across to such good effect that after her death in May 1791, not a single one of her votaries would either straighten or dress the corpse. And nor would they coffin her until obliged to do so by the offending smell by then emanating from the 'undead' Buchanite leader. Even then, and faithful to the end, they still refused to bury her in the ground, but instead built up the coffin in a corner of the barn which served as their Tabernacle. They daily expected that, true to her promised word, Elspith would rise again and lead them off to the Promised Land.

Finally, it was left to neighbouring country people, thoroughly disgusted and shocked by such proceedings, to go to a Justice of the Peace and ask for help. They were granted an order that she should be buried and that without delay. In this way, the 'undead' woman was committed to the ground and as 'dust to dust, ashes to ashes', joined others who had gone the way of all flesh at the end of their allotted span.

It is not the purpose of this chapter to draw comparisons between the Buchanite sect and other such religious fanatical groups which have sprung up worldwide over the years. Even so, and in light of the recent horrendous events in Texas, U.S.A., it must surely give the reader food for thought!

JEAN ADAM (1710 - 1765)

One of Life's Losers

Why is it that some people, get all the raw deals in life? And no matter what they do or how hard they try to better themselves, things just never seem to turn out right for them.

Such a one was Jean Adam, a Scottish poetess who was born in 1710 at Crawfordsdyke, a parish of Greenock in Renfrewshire. The daughter of a fairly prosperous Shipmaster, young Jean might well have expected an easy start in life and a cushioned existence far removed from the pathetic paupers she saw all around her in the Greenock of that day and age.

However, it was not to be, for she was orphaned as a young child, and the moment that she was of an age to earn a living, she entered into service. Her first post was that of housemaid-cum-nursery Governess in the home of the Rev. Mr. Turner, a Greenock Minister. She was fortunate in her position in this caring family, for it was not all work and drudgery, as might have been expected, and even better still, the young housemaid was allowed the use of the Manse library. This was a real boon and so in whatever free time she had, young Jean made full use of this facility. In this way, not only did she manage to give herself a pretty fair education, but she also took the opportunity in the peace and quiet of the library, far removed from the noise of the nursery, to start writing some poetry.

Eventually, she had written so many poems that a helpful friend of the family, a Mrs. Drummond, also of Greenock, collected and published them for her in 1734. As part of this project the young housemaid/Governess changed to the pseudonym of Mrs Jane Adams. The work was entitled: 'MISCELLANY POEMS by Mrs JANE ADAMS in CRAWFORDSDYKE', Glasgow, 1734.

It was published by subscription and a list of the gentry, merchants and Ministers who had subscribed was given in the book. Jean's poetry must have been quite highly regarded at that point for the number of people on the subscribers list came to 154.

The young poetess dedicated her poems to 'Thomas Crawford of Crawfordburn' and a Mr. Archibald Crawford wrote the preface. A copy, if it were to be found today, would doubtless be something of a collector's item. There is at least one anomaly in the book. Although complete with index and promised to be in two parts, one 'all in meeter' and the other in 'blank verse in imitation of Milton'; the amazing thing is that there is in fact no blank verse to be found anywhere in the book. One can only suppose that either the young poetess ran out of ideas... or they lacked a good proof-reader. It appears that Jean, quite happy to blow her own trumpet, had suggested that her poems which incidentally were all religious in theme, were written 'in the style of the best English poets that have written within seventy years.' Despite this spot of self-advertising, the general opinion seemed to be that the religious poems of the young authoress were 'poor specimens indeed.'

The young poetess dedicated her poems to 'Thomas Crawford of Crawfordburn'

Whatever of that, at least the ordered 154 copies had been sold. So, fired by the 'success' of her book, Jean Adam then decided to quit service and instead set up a girls' school. Ambitious project this may have been for the inexperienced Jean Adam, but strangely enough, in no time at all, influential parents started flocking to enrol their daughters. Perhaps it was the cachet of her having had a volume of religious poetry published, or perhaps a good word from her former employer which did the trick, but whatever the reason, Jean's school for girls became an instant success. And it continued to do well, this perhaps on account of her 'modern' teaching methods. As well as teaching the basic three R's, the innovative young Headmistress, also varied the daily routine when she gave spirited Shakespearean readings to her entranced pupils. History has it that 'according to tradition, she swooned with excitement while reading scenes from 'Othello'.'

So far so good then. Life seemed to be going well for Jean Adam and to date there had been no indication of the later hell which awaited her. Just at that point, her book of Collected poems had sold well to the subscribers, albeit with little monetary gains to the author, and her school seemed to be going from strength to strength. Perhaps if she had been persuaded to leave things at that, then all would have been well? Who knows?

What is established fact is that rather than try to sell the remaining copies of her book in Greenock where she was already well-known and respected as a Headmistress, Jean decided on a different approach. Quite out of the blue she went to the expense of shipping out her unsold copies to Boston, of all places ... and they were never heard of again. Why Boston, one asks? Perhaps there just happened to be a ship loading in Greenock for that particular American port at that moment ... and it seemed like a good idea at the time! Whatever of that, the remaining copies vanished into limbo, and so closed a chapter in Jean's life.

Meantime, Jean continued with her school, but rather than build on its already established success, for some reason best known to herself, she went off at a tangent. What exactly did she do?

During the course of her literary recitations to her pupils, Jean had decided that her idol was the 'CLARISSA' of Richardson. That being so, she decided in her wisdom and against all friendly advice, that nothing would do but that she would close the school for six weeks, while she herself would travel to London, there to meet with the author. Not only did she realise this ambition, but perhaps her greatest achievement was the fact that she travelled on foot the entire distance from Greenock in Scotland to London.

In that day and age it would normally take about seventeen or eighteen days to make the journey from Glasgow to London by coach.

Not only was it considered to be a very dangerous journey but the cost of around seven pounds equated with more money than a male servant would earn in an entire year. It would appear from this that Jean did not have sufficient money saved from her school to be able to afford the coach fare. Or perhaps even then, she looked on the project of going on foot to London as the great adventure of her life. Whatever the reason, one thing was crystal clear - she was desperate to get to 'Lunnun.'

This remarkable journey possibly gave her a feeling of wanderlust. In any case, she was soon 'compelled to give up her school' - perhaps the parents of her pupils did not take too kindly to her by now somewhat erratic behaviour?

With her school once disbanded, her remaining volumes of poetry lost somewhere on the high seas between Greenock and America, the soured and disappointed woman became a wanderer. As she trailed about from one part of Scotland to another, she eventually became a hawker, trying to scrape up enough to live on with her modest sales of trinkets, ribbons and chap-books. It is doubtful if she made any more of a success at this latest venture.

What is known is that towards the end of her life, she again turned up in her home-town of Greenock. By now in a very distressed, filthy and under-nourished state, it was clear that she needed help and that quickly. An Order of the Bailies of the town caused her to be admitted to the Glasgow Poorhouse. They described her to the Poorhouse authorities as 'a poor woman in distress; a stranger who has been wandering abroad.'

The terrible irony of her admittance to the Glasgow Poorhouse is that for a woman who had obviously loved the fresh air and the freedom of her nomadic lifestyle, she died the very next day, 3rd April, 1765, in the overcrowded, comfortless and stinking Workhouse.

And the last official word we have of poor Jean is that 'she was buried at the House expense'. In other words, a pauper's funeral would be the last rites accorded to Jean Adam. And what exactly did this mean in the year 1765? Sometimes a 'stranger's chest' would cost no more than around one and sixpence and this small amount of money meant the corpse had only 'a wee len o' the burial chest'. What happened was that the body would be borne in the 'chest' to the burial place, and buried only in the winding-sheet. When the workhouse or Parish chest was about halfway down into the grave, holding bolts would be drawn, and the body would fall through the bottom into the waiting earth.

Had her life's story ended there, it would have been tragic enough. But Jean Adam left behind her a very large and much-argued literary question-mark. It has been said that 'her only passport to fame is the claim so persistently asserted for her of the authorship of the 'SONG OF THE MARINER'S WIFE', otherwise more commonly known as 'THERE'S NAE LUCK ABOOT THE HOOSE.' This song has in turn been described as being 'one of the sweetest in any language' with its humorous, simple and touching lyric. Controversy as to the true authorship has raged for centuries and has never yet been finally accorded. History tells us that a copy of it in his own handwriting was found among the papers of the poet Julius Mickle who died in 1788. In 'THE NEW NATIONAL SONG BOOK' (Boosey & Hawkes 1955) the song 'THERE'S NAE LUCK ABOUT THE HOUSE' is 'attributed to Julius Mickle' with a footnote to the effect that the fifth stanza, beginning 'Sae true his heart, sae smooth his speech' was added by Dr. James Beattie, author of 'THE MINSTREL.'

It might be worth-while at this stage examining the claims of Julius Mickle and Jean Adam respectively. Apart from the fact of a copy of the song having been found among Mickle's papers, there were other plus factors in his favour. It was generally felt that since he had 'a fertile imagination and power of rich and varied versification, and wrote very good songs and ballads,' it was entirely logical that 'a counterclaim has been set up for him.' Be that as it may, and if true that he did in fact write the disputed verses, there is still one unexplained mystery ... is it not rather strange that never once did Mickle include the disputed verses in the Collections of all his other poems throughout his lifetime? No explanation of this anomaly has ever been proffered.

And what are the reasons and thinking behind the claim that Jean Adam wrote the disputed song? This is where the mystery deepens even more. History records for us the fact that the poem, as it then was, was hawked for sale in the streets of Greenock somewhere round 1772, fully seven years after Jean Adam's death. It eventually found a place in Herd's 1776 Collection and also in 1778 in 'The NIGHTINGALE'. Further to this, it was former pupils of Jean Adam who insisted that their then respected Headmistress had recited the poem to them, and it is worth noting that this time to which they referred was then all of forty years previously.

To the student of history, there are several other points which may or may not point to the fact of Jean Adam's being the true author. Not only did her former pupils remember the poem, they were also convinced that it had been of her own composition. Add to that the fact that tradition has it that it was written about Colin and Jean Campbell, a couple from Crawfordsdyke, which of course was the home area of Jean Adam. But even this was not enough evidence to convince those people who thought it utterly ridiculous that Jean Adam could have been the author. They held to the view that 'it is unlikely that such a strain of home and married love could have been written by this wayward and unwedded woman.' On the other hand, perhaps it is not without significance that poor wanderer and hawker as she had become in later life, Jean Adam was originally from a good home. Even more apposite, her father had been a respected Shipmaster, and as such, often away from home. So no doubt to Jean and her mother, it was all too often perfectly true that there was 'nae luck aboot the hoose when oor gudeman's awa.' Following this line, although the poem may have been about two entirely different people, might not the distant memory of a home without the 'gudeman' have influenced the poet? For all we know, and assuming Jean Adam to have been the author, might not the poignant poem have been written out of a longing for a settled home-life, married bliss and all the domestic comforts which had so cruelly been denied the 'stranger who has been wandering abroad?'

A Historian, writing of this great literary mystery, said in his conclusion in a paper of 1885: 'And of all the seven verses now always given in this poem, whoever wrote the main body of the work, one thing is certain - the last two verses are known to have been written and added by Dr. Blair.' There again we have a slight problem as to authorship for the fifth verse, as we have already seen, has been attributed to another doctor, one Dr. James Beattie. And up to 1885, no mention that anyone other than the original poet had written the first five verses!

That then is the story of Jean Adam, a Scottish poetess, definitely one of life's losers ... in the end she had neither family, friend, goods and chattel, nor even a coffin to call her own. And what may have been her greatest achievement, a poem sung by Scots in whatever far-flung outpost of the world they may be ... not even that has been accredited to her.

'Nae luck aboot the hoose?' Those well-chosen words could all too easily have been written by, for and about the luckless Jean Adam... for whom in the end, the only hoose was that of the Glasgow Poorhouse.

MIRANDA BARRY STUART

Otherwise known as Dr James Barry

As a general rule, the vast majority of Scottish women of the late 18th and early 19th centuries were homemakers to the extent that whatever ambitions they had harboured to 'get on in life' they tended to foist on to their male offspring.

But there was one Scottish woman who, although born in 1795, did not fit the common mould. Early on in life she decided that she would dress as a man, train to be a doctor, and that having done so, the world would then be her oyster.

Who was this woman? Where did she spring from? And what other idiosyncrasies did she display?

Her parentage, birthplace and early days are all something of a grey area. It is thought that her parents were Scottish, although one or two versions have it that her father was a General Miranda, with her mother alone being Scottish. She is believed to have been born in or around London, with her early childhood being spent at various places in England. Despite this, such history books as do mention her, seem to have claimed Miranda Barry Stuart as Scotland's own, to the extent that she is then referred to as James Barry, a Scottish doctor.

Our first sighting of this remarkable character from Scotland's past is when at the age of fifteen she started to dress as a man. Then, having studied for the requisite period at Edinburgh University, where it was rumoured that her patron was the Earl of Buchan, she qualified as a doctor.

As if this in itself were not sufficient achievement for a young woman of the time, she went on to join the British Army, for which she managed to pass the necessary examinations -- one can only hazard a guess that such examinations were to assess her suitability as an Army doctor, rather than any physical examination. Whatever of that, in 1816, with her promotion to Army Staff Surgeon confirmed, she was sent out to join a unit in South Africa, then called the Cape Colony. No sooner had she arrived there than she started making herself very unpopular with those in authority. Even at that early age, it appears from various reports that she was irascible, difficult to approach, and would not suffer fools, bumbledom nor officialdom gladly. In fact, the rest of her life seems to have been a series of confrontations of one kind or another with superior officers and pen-pushers, followed by a hasty transfer and quickly arranged promotion to some other, and preferably more remote, part of the world. Perhaps the reasoning was that the higher she got in the Army's service, the less of a nuisance factor to the authorities would be the young doctor. The reality was that nothing could have been further from the truth!

The year 1821 found her as Colonial Medical Inspector, more unpopular than ever, and true to form, still denouncing, investigating and setting inquiries into the state of Leper Colonies, a variety of Public Jails, and other such places and minority groups already dear to the heart of Dr. James Barry.

Always a very direct person, Dr. Barry was also noted for virulent letters in which she castigated officialdom and/or whoever happened to be in charge of the various places where she found appalling conditions. She was also loud and prolific in her adverse comments as to countless matters relating to conduct and official doctrine and principles with which she did not agree. So it is not altogether surprising to learn that in 1827 the irritable doctor was on her travels again, this time to Mauritius. Four years later, and no doubt leaving behind her the usual trail of complaints and unanswered letters, she was on her way yet again, on this occasion to Jamaica. Things must have been slightly better there, for this time the tour of duty lasted a record five years.

Dr. Barry next turns up on the island of St. Helena, her designation that of Principal Medical Officer. As has already been seen, Doctor Barry was ever a 'bonnie fechter', and true to form, was soon again at loggerheads with the local authorities. The causus belli this time? She organised a campaign on behalf of the women of St. Helena, demanding that they receive whatever medical treatment they required in a separate building which she insisted should be well away from the main barracks.

History tells us that a large number of these women were suffering from V.D., so perhaps the normally irate Dr. Barry did feel some compassion for these women, and appreciated that they did deserve some small measure of privacy. Perhaps this latest campaign did not meet with the approval of the men in authority -- after all, they did not have Dr. Barry's advantage of exercising womanly instincts and compassion for suffering members of her own sex. Who knows exactly what further confrontations followed? All that can be said with any degree of certainty at this distance in time is that a year or so later, Dr. Barry had left St. Helena, its underprivileged women and its assorted problems behind her and was again getting into verbal battle in yet another region of the world.

It should be pointed out that throughout her career of Army doctoring and constant battling for justice -- or what she herself perceived of as justice -- for minority groups of one kind or another, Dr. James Barry was always thought to be a man. So complete was her disguise and so 'manly' her conduct and brusque manner that never once was her secret even suspected. That situation was about to change.

Once settled in her usual fashion in her latest posting to Trinidad and at a date sometime before 1845, she fell victim to extremely severe bouts of yellow fever. In fact, so close to death did she come on several occasions that in the course of her essential treatment it dawned on her astounded medical adviser that his patient was, in fact, a woman. Before she was completely restored to health, two assistant surgeons became privy to the knowledge of Dr. James Barry's real sex. However, perhaps they too, like so many before them, were in awe of the renowned 'Battling Barry', and feared to 'get the worst word out of her stomach,' or even, on her recovery one of her famous 'stiff letters'. Whatever the reason, they kept the amazing secret strictly to themselves. It does occur to one that perhaps another reason for their enforced silence lay in the fact that Dr. James Barry always had a 'minder' with her, no matter where she travelled. This companion, who kept as close to her as her own shadow, was a giant of a man, a Negro who answered to the name of Sambo. The oddly-assorted pair were also accompanied at all times by the Doctor's small dog called Psyche. Her two companions may or may not have acted as a deterrent to anyone wishing to denounce her as a fraud. Anyway, the end result was that in time not only did Dr. Barry survive this close shave with discovery, but she regained her health to the point where, in 1858, she was again off on her travels. Having been made Inspector General of Hospitals, in this capacity she travelled to and worked in Canada.

After a year's work in Canada, where no doubt she kept up her usual strict standards and ongoing compassion for underprivileged minority groups, she decided that she had finally had quite enough of world travel.

So, then aged 64 years, she elected to return to Britain, where in London she spent the rest of her life until her death in 1865.

She had done the impossible then? Kept her amazing and well-guarded secret to the end? Well, not quite! Knowing that her last days on earth were imminent, Dr. James Barry, organised to the last and ever punctilious, left explicit instructions that 'he' was to be buried without prior examination of the body, and of course, had this last will and testament been carried out to the letter, then naturally it would have followed that Dr. James Barry's lifetime secret would have gone with 'him' to the grave.

Alas, it was not to be. 'His' wishes were totally ignored. And so it was discovered, to the amazement of all concerned, that the much-travelled and ever-irascible Dr. James Barry had in fact been a woman.

Even more astounding, and what caused a sensation when the news was announced: Dr. James Barry had obviously borne a child at some early part of 'his' life!

Truly one of the great eccentrics of Scotland's past, Miranda Barry Stuart may have been a mother, but she was not one of the inestimable breed of Scotswomen who abnegated their own ambitions in favour of their male off-spring. Neither did she, like those morally tough and physically strong women, spend her life in washing, ironing, making broth, cooking the parritch, baking the tattie scones and rearing her children to 'better themselves and get on in life'.

Instead Miranda Barry Stuart knew exactly what she herself wanted out of life -- to dress as a man, train to be a doctor and travel the world spreading her own brand of justice for the underprivileged, be they lepers, prisoners or other women.

Eccentric she may have been, unapproachable and irascible, and unbowing to bumbledom and those in authority she most certainly was, and yet one thing stands clear above all else:

Miranda Barry Stuart did exactly what she had set out to do with her allotted span. Not only that, but as well as living her life, in the way she wanted, she not only defied convention, she kept her well-guarded secret almost to the end.

For her achievements alone, not to mention her skill and expertise as a doctor in the farthest-flung outposts of the world, she has surely earned her place in the pages of Scottish history.

THE INVERGORDON MUTINY
September 14th 1931

On September 14th, 1996, it was the 65th Anniversary of an historic event which although hushed up and kept under such a cloak of secrecy at the time of its happening that it caused little or no interest, far less scandal, in Britain, it nevertheless caused rampant panic abroad in banking circles. And although the men involved themselves referred to the event as nothing more than 'a strike', it has come down in history - that is, where it is given a brief mention at all - as: 'THE INVERGORDON MUTINY.'

To understand the cause of this naval mutiny, we must first take a look at the social and economic conditions then prevailing in Britain. Between the years 1930 and 1931, the rate of unemployment was escalating until by the end of July 1931 it stood at the record 2.7 million of the population.

And throughout the land, dispirited groups of unemployed men in their 'uniform' of cloth caps, mufflers and thin hand-me-down suits, wandered from street-corner to street-corner. These unfortunate men had nothing in the way of material goods or comforts, they were going nowhere, there wasn't a glimmer of hope as regards gainful employment on the horizon, and ill-nourishment, despair and disillusion stared out from their haunted eyes.

Occasionally, in a frantic bid to earn a few pennies, a man would break away from the group. Then, with upturned cap in hand, he would wander round the back-courts of the many tenements, there to give a soulful rendition of 'THE OLD RUGGED CROSS.' If he happened to strike it lucky, then a few coppers or even a skilfully-aimed jeely-piece would be thrown down to him from a kindly, but equally impoverished, housewife who had been washing either the dishes or her weans at the jaw-boax by the window.

On other less auspicious occasions, and especially if his rendition of the well-loved hymn happened to be about the thirtieth rendering the captive audience had heard on that particular day, then casement windows would be slammed shut in disgust ... but not before a torrent of verbal abuse and the bandying-about of a few well-chosen Scottish phrases and four-letter words.

And in the City streets themselves, small bands of unemployed ex-servicemen trailed along the gutters, all the while playing drums, bagpipes or failing that, a rusty cornet or perhaps even a comb and paper. Meanwhile, on every street corner, other hopefuls would be trying to sell matches and home-made toys, or even executing as spirited a knee-and-spoon routine as their undernourished state would allow.

The summer of 1931 dragged on, and the aura of despair was not in the least helped by the onset of the U.K's most violent earthquake on record on June 7th, when severe earth-tremors were felt throughout the land, all the way from the English Channel to the farthest-flung Highlands of Scotland.

By the end of July, with unemployment figures still soaring towards the three million mark, a special Economy Committee was set up under the leadership of Sir George May, the former Secretary of Prudential Assurance. He recommended that not only should substantial Income Tax increases be implemented, there should also be immediate salary cuts for teachers, police and all the armed forces. He further recommended that the dole-money should be cut and this measure together with the other swingeing cut-backs would enable the Government to make a saving of £96 million in a year.

As conditions throughout the entire United Kingdom steadily worsened, the then Chancellor of the Exchequer Philip Snowden, went into action with his Emergency Budget on 11th September. There would be a penny a pint on beer; sixpence on the Income Tax; Dole money was to be cut from 17 shillings to 15 shillings-and-threepence; teachers' pay would be reduced by 15%; and perhaps the most drastic cuts of all were to be for the Armed Forces. This meant that all servicemen had their pay cut by as much as 25% in a bid "to stop the country living beyond its means."

Although these measures were to take effect immediately, with regard to the Air Force, Army, Navy and the Police Force, there were those who felt that news of the cuts was deliberately delayed until they were safely out of harm's way. Such a group were the 12,000 or so ratings on 15 ships of the Atlantic Fleet at their isolated base of Invergordon. Not only were they enraged when they realised that with the new pay rates, a great many men would be left with only about twenty-five shillings per week, they felt that they had been 'conned'. Yes! What really angered them and roused them to protest was the view that the powers-that-be had made sure they were well away from home ports and other such navy towns as Portsmouth before full details of their swingeing pay cuts were revealed. The general feeling was that obviously much greater impact and havoc could have been caused in a busy port, but up in the wilds of Invergordon, little harm could result from the disenchanted mariners.

ratings of the Atlantic Fleet categorically refused to put to sea

Three days after the pay-cuts had come into operation, the ratings of the warship, 'VALIANT', led by Able-Seaman Len Wincott, took occupation of a shore canteen and also met for protest-meetings on a recreation ground. The upshot was that this small group of men, by now joined by many others of their 12,000 ratings colleagues of the Atlantic Fleet, categorically refused to put to sea. And it is important to note at this point, that the protesters referred to their action as 'a strike' rather than a full-blown mutiny. In addition to their refusal to put to sea, they further ignored the traditional Naval command of "On the Knee!", thereby refusing to obey or even listen to any words of command or advice from their superior officers.

Despite the fact that the 'striking' ratings had access to a supply of firearms, violence was kept deliberately low-key... Some of the officers were locked in their cabins by their subordinates; there were a few broken windows ashore; and a thrown beer-glass dealt a glancing blow and cut an officer's head. Altogether, it appeared to be a fairly 'gentlemanly, we-in-Britain' type of protest, even to the extent that when some rather over-exuberant ratings started singing 'The Red Flag', they were thought to be out of order and were howled down by their more mannerly shipmates! They then substituted a well-known and popular drinking song, "The More We are Together, the Merrier We Shall Be." And over the next few days of the 'strike', this became their theme-tune.

As the 'strike' daily gained in momentum towards becoming a full-blown mutiny, one particular Admiral-of-the-Fleet, noted for his sense of humour, is reputed to have sent the following message:
'PRO BONO PUBLICO, NO RUDDY PANICO.'

This may or may not have been true or if so, perhaps it did help to diffuse the situation somewhat. What is known is that by now the striking sailors had got themselves fairly well-organised and had re-affirmed their boast that above all, this would be a polite strike/mutiny in the course of which, if it could be possibly avoided, not one person would be either physically hurt or molested in any way. Thus fully determined to do things 'properly', they also instituted their own daily ritual of saluting the White Ensign. And apart from, as has already been noted, locking some officers in their cabins, they accorded a measure of politeness to their superior officers, for whom the usual customary respect was observed.

The ground rules well and truly laid, their next step was to send their Manifesto to the Admiralty. This read:

"We, the loyal subjects of His Majesty the King, do hereby present to our Lords the Commissioners of the Admiralty our representation and implore them to amend the drastic cuts in pay which have been inflicted on the lowest-paid men of the lower-deck. It is evident to all concerned that these cuts are a fore-runner of tragedy, misery and immorality among the families of the lower deck, and unless a guaranteed written agreement is received from the Admiralty, confirmed by Parliament, stating that our pay will be revised, we are still to remain as one unit, refusing to serve under the new rates of pay. The men are quite agreeable to accept a cut which they consider within reason."

One rating was quoted as saying;

"Cuts like this will lead our wives and families to starvation. The only hope of survival would be for our wives to turn to prostitution."

Yet another rating told a reporter:

"We are fighting for our wives and children. The cuts can't hit us on board ship. We've cut out the luxuries long ago. Our wives, after the rent is paid, have no more than a pound. How can they stand a cut of seven and sixpence?"

The Coalition Government, terrified that the whole country would erupt into violent protests, should news of the mutiny leak out, did its level best to hush up the whole affair. And where it got any mention at all in newspapers of the day, it was merely referred to as some very minor local difficulty in His Majesty's Navy at Invergordon in the North of Scotland.

As part of its policy of keeping the lid on the Invergordon Mutiny, eventually the Admiralty sailed all the men from the mutinous ships to their home ports. Once there, the 'striking' crews were disbanded, some ratings were sacked from the Service and it is known that at least one rating, thoroughly disgruntled with the prevailing social and economic conditions in Britain, took himself off at high speed to Moscow!

Thus, in this way, little or no scandal was caused in its country of origin by the Invergordon Mutiny. However, it must be said that despite the best efforts of the British Government and the Lords of the Admiralty to strangle at birth any reports of their 'little local difficulty in the Navy', they could still do nothing about the garbled rumours which reached the foreign press. Not only were these written up in foreign newspapers, the many weird rumours were exaggerated to such an extent that people abroad were led to believe that a bloody Revolution, almost on the scale of the French Revolution, had started in Britain!

This in turn led foreign investors to believe that Great Britain was on the brink of ruin and in the ongoing snowball effect of such things, this panic belief led to a massive run on the gold reserves of the Bank of England. The end result of this was that the Government realised that the Mutiny must be dealt with not only quickly, but reasonably, mildly and in as low-key a manner as was possible in the circumstances.

As has already been noted, somewhere around 24 ratings were dismissed from the Service, but despite their handling the affair with kid gloves, the Lords of the Admiralty were the first to admit that the damage had already been done, not only to the Bank of England but also to the previously prestigious name of Great Britain as a world-power.

An interesting footnote is that so successful was the attempt to squash all record of the Mutiny that even today, more than half a century later, the serious student of history will find little or no mention of this historic event in reference books. Indeed, many newspapers of the day in reporting that Britain had come off the Gold Standard did not state the true reason for this i.e. the panic abroad caused by the fact of the Invergordon Mutiny in Scotland. Rather, they took the line of trying to re-assure the citizens of Britain that there was "no cause for alarm."

In a leading article in 'THE ROTHESAY EXPRESS' on 22nd September, just eight days after the events up in the area around the Cromarty Firth, not a single mention of the Mutiny, but rather a hammering-home of the message that "There is no need to be panicky. There is no -shortage of food, clothing, labour, or any of the necessities of life. The present situation is not caused by famine, earthquake or fire. It is an artificial one which can be turned to good account by the exercise of wise statesmanship on the part of our legislators."

The patriotic writer went on:

"As a whole, we will be forced to live more within our own resources, spend less on imported luxuries, and buy the manufactures and raw materials of our own Empire, which are more than sufficient to protect us against want."

And the student of history will be particularly interested in the following bit of propaganda:

"The position of British banks and banking is as solid as ever, and there is no cause for anxiety on that score. The international situation, which has caused the breakdown of normal means of exchange, is due partly to the war, and the failure of countries abroad to meet their obligations."

On another page of the same issue of 'THE ROTHESAY EXPRESS', a local poet had been inspired to give his thoughts on the Emergency Budget:

I PAY, YOU PAY, WE ALL PAY.
The Government, with good intent,
Has tapped the country's sources,
Phil Snowden's pill has left us ill,
-Our job "To Pay", of course is.
At first we hear we pay on beer,
And doubtless hard we think it,
The penny more, we part with sore,
But we have to grin and drink it.

by CLIPY

No doubt the sentiments expressed in this poem would have been heartily endorsed by the many unemployed throughout Britain. It is only fair to record that thanks to their 'striking' efforts at Invergordon, the ratings had their pay-cuts partially restored, but despite this, they were still more than 10% Also, this figure applied to all workers in the Public Service, including police and teachers. And in a desperate bid to restore a measure of trust, the Coalition Cabinet even went so far as to make the gesture of cutting their own salaries by 20%.

A month after the Invergordon Mutiny, posters for the General Election of October 1931 started appearing on billboards. These striking posters depicted a worried-looking mother in an overall, with a crying child in her arms and a clinging, undernourished-looking toddler on her arm. This pathetic trio were set against a background of smoke-free factory chimneys and deserted mines, while in the foreground was an army of gaunt and bunneted, obviously out-of-work men. The caption at the top of the poster read:

"Smokeless chimneys and - ANXIOUS MOTHERS."

And the foot of the poster carried the banner headline:

"The Remedy - Vote for the NATIONAL GOVERNMENT."

Such a vivid poster certainly got the message home about poverty, undernourishment and the ongoing worry of mass unemployment...

It must be said that the instigators and participants of the Invergordon Mutiny also got their grievances across with excellent and immediate effect, to those in Governmental power ... and all that, despite the heavy blanket of censorship which was at once thrown over the event.

THE SCOTTISH INSURRECTION OF 1820
& THE BATTLE OF BONNYMUIR

On April 1st, 1996 it was the 176th anniversary of a notable event in our nation's history - the Scottish Insurrection of 1820. And although this event and its brave leaders nowadays receive but scant attention in the history books, the anniversary of this particular Scottish Memory should not be allowed to pass un-noticed into the mists of time.

That being so, let's take a closer look ... what exactly was the Scottish Insurrection? Who were its martyrs? Where did it take place? What was the time-table of events? And finally what effect did it have on later historical happenings not only in Scotland, but also in such far-flung places as America, Australia, Canada and New Zealand?

Before we can state exactly what the Scottish Insurrection was, it is necessary to take a look at the social and economic climate then prevailing throughout Great Britain.

The year 1819 had been a time of social unrest and economic discontent among the workers, the unemployed and disenchanted returning-soldiers. Despite the fact that fortunes were then being made by factory, land and coal-mining owners and that these very same fortunes came from the sweat and toil of the workers, nevertheless, members of the working-class themselves were regarded as the lowest of the low, the scum of the earth, the vile, stinking, un-educated 'great un-washed'. And if they tried to voice a protest, dared to hope for better working conditions, decent wages or even a dreamed-of release from their rat-infested hovels, then at once they were howled down by their affluent and comfortably-housed 'social superiors', more commonly referred to as their 'betters.'

The protest meetings, demonstrations, marches and summer of discontent culminated in the massacre of Peterloo. This happened on August 16th, 1819 when a relatively peaceful and unarmed crowd of workers and the unemployed converged on St. Peter's Fields, Manchester. More than 60,000 people attended the demonstration and scarcely had the meeting begun and they were listening avidly to Henry Hunt, a Radical speaker, when all hell broke loose. Although unarmed, it had been noticed by those in authority that a number of the 'great unwashed' were carrying sticks. While it was perfectly in order for any gentleman to carry a cane, this was most certainly not the case for the lower orders of society. That being so, and under the guise of ostensibly arresting Henry Hunt and his platform party of followers, the magistrates of Manchester ordered that the local yeomanry should immediately, and with drawn swords, charge into the unsuspecting crowd.

The result of this bloody massacre was that it left many hundreds of innocent bystanders shocked and stunned, over four hundred people horribly injured and eleven other unfortunate members of the public killed - either sabred or trampled to death in the ensuing mêlée.

When the full horror of the Peterloo Massacre became generally known, at first there was shocked disbelief, closely followed by wide repercussions throughout the country, and not least in Scotland.

One of the first of these was a demonstration in Paisley on Saturday, September 11th. On that day and from early morning, crowds of weavers, miners, and the unemployed streamed into Paisley from such places as Ayr, Dalry, Galston, Glasgow, Johnstone, Kilbarchan, Kilmarnock and Strathaven.

And as a mark of respect to the fallen of Peterloo, not only were the Radical flags edged in black, so also were the members of the demonstration committee and many other sympathisers dressed in the sombre black of deep mourning. And for those impoverished souls who could not afford any clothing other than their normal workaday garb, they, almost to a man, wore either a black band or a diamond-of-black stitched to ragged sleeves.

What had more or less come to be regarded as the Scottish National Anthem, 'SCOTS WHA HAE' was played by a band from Neilston. The crowd of some 18,000-strong listened to impassioned speeches from a number of Radicals, one of whom, Alexander Taylor, a local schoolmaster, also chaired the meeting. He was able to inform his audience of the vast support already rallying throughout Scotland for the Radical cause, and not least of which was the offer of a Glasgow printer, William Lang, who had kindly offered his help and expertise in the printing and publishing of a Scottish Radical newspaper. Before the close of the meeting, money was collected for the benefit of those relatives of the victims of the Peterloo Massacre. The meeting broke up without incident in the early evening and as they trudged their several ways homeward, no doubt the miners, weavers and the unemployed Radical sympathisers felt relieved that the events of Peterloo had not been re-enacted, this time in a Scottish field.

However, their self-congratulation that history had not in fact repeated itself was to be short-lived. Making their way back into Paisley, it was at once apparent that a great number of special constables had been situated in strategic places the length of the High Street and right up to the outside of the Saracen's Head Inn. The Glasgow contingent of over three hundred men swerved neither to the left nor right, neither did they attempt to escape like rats down any vennels, backcourt or side-streets. Rather, with the stirring words of their leaders still ringing in their ears, they marched the more proudly, with heads held high, shoulders back and their Radical flags and banners waving proudly in the evening breeze. In this manner all went well until, on reaching the Cross, Oliver Jamieson, the Lord Provost of Paisley, angrily went forward and attempted to seize one of the black-edged Radical flags.

This rash act was enough to spark off something of a mêlée in which stones, sticks and other missiles were thrown at the police. One thing borrowed another, an upstanding citizen from Gateside complained to James Brown, the Paisley Police Superintendent that not only had he been knocked down in the scuffle, he had also been robbed; and before long the fighting had escalated to such a point that not only was the Council Chambers under attack, the whole town of Paisley erupted into a seething cauldron of angry, yelling, fighting mobs.

The end result of that day's efforts was that there was much damage to property in the way of smashed windows, torn-up iron railings, and stone-littered streets; not a few bloodied noses and sore heads; and finally at ten o'clock, when the streets had still not been cleared of rioters, it was found necessary to read the Riot Act, after which cavalry reinforcements were urgently called in from Glasgow.

Even so, it was to be well into the 'wee, sma' hoors' before anything even remotely resembling an uneasy calm descended on Paisley, when the only sound then to be heard, was that of troops of the 10th Hussars still galloping through the town.

For the rest of that troubled Autumn and Winter throughout the central belt of Scotland there were sporadic outbursts of Radical protest, mob-rule and a subsequent strict curfew in Paisley; the arrest at Airdrie of a band with the temerity to play the by-now forbidden 'SCOTS WHA HAE'; a large Radical rally at Linktown of Kirkcaldy at which close on 6,000 people heard a Mr. Mitchell read out a detailed document of some fourteen resolutions, all of which were adopted; at a meeting in Paisley, the chairman placed on his head the Cap of Liberty, the symbol of the French Revolution; raids in the tenements of Glasgow resulted in many arrests; and altogether it was abundantly clear that the 'common herd' were decidedly unhappy with their lot.

The then Government was quick to realise the extent of militant and Radical feeling throughout the country and the Ministers of the Crown knew that something must be done - and that quickly. So it was, almost in a state of panic that they introduced something called the Six Acts, which were in effect, nothing other than an iron-fisted mode of severely repressive legislation.

In addition to the publicly declared Six Acts, the Government took the opportunity further to strengthen its hidden, underground network of spies. For all the while that Radical activity and civil disobedience was escalating in Scotland, unbeknown to the Radicals themselves was the fact that the Government was also hard at work, in building up and establishing an insidious network of spies, dupes of spies and 'agents provocateurs.'

The depth of anger, frustration and despair on all sides deepened, especially after the arrest of 27 members of a Radical Committee in Glasgow, on suspicion of their supposedly planning an uprising. This development, of course, only made matters worse, especially when common rumour had it that the incipient uprising was scheduled to take place simultaneously in Scotland and in England.

It was therefore no surprise to anyone - the discontented weavers of Paisley, the 'great unwashed' in general or even their employers, factors, lords and masters, 'betters', one and all, when on April 1st 1820, a Proclamation appeared on the walls of houses, tenements and factories.

And with the posting of that Proclamation, a new, exciting and horrendously dangerous chapter of cloak-and-dagger politics and hand-to-hand fighting between master and servant was about to begin. Scotland would never be the same again. Nor for that matter would many another country far beyond auld Scotia's 'Bonnie Banks.'

History was in the making, but the events of those years of public unrest were so horrific, so mind-boggling that over time, all knowledge of them was swept under the carpet, hidden from public view. It is the purpose of this chapter to bring them out into the light of day, there to examine in detail the daring deeds perpetrated by our ancestors in the cause of personal freedom ...

And what better time to honour these brave martyrs, and all they stood for, than on the 176th anniversary of the Scottish Insurrection?

THE PROCLAMATION

The Proclamation, signed 1st April, 1820 and posted during the hours of darkness suddenly appeared like a rash on the walls of houses, tenements, factories throughout Scotland in such places as Ayr, Dumbarton, Glasgow, Lanark, Renfrew, Stirling and even in many a tiny village.

Signed by the 'Committee of Organisation for forming a Provisional Government', the Proclamation called the workers of Scotland not only to take part in a national strike, but also to rise up in arms against authority and all it stood for. The unequivocal motto was 'LIBERTY OR DEATH'. And lest any reader of the Proclamation should still be in doubt, it was further spelled out ... "We have sworn to return home in triumph or return no more."

Picture the scene, as word of the momentous happening spread, gradually the early-morning streets began to fill with bunnetted, muffled workers, the ragged unemployed and pale women beshawled with bairns happed up in shawls, women who were old before their time with the double burden of too many children and too little money or food. Those unable to read hung on the words laboriously spelled out by the more educated among them.

Then as the full realisation of the emotive words began to sink in, the street crowds graduated to mobs. And these in turn, casting about for ways in which to vent their spleen, started hurling abuse, rotten fruit and stones at any passing well-dressed citizen, prosperous-looking businessman, or best of all, any uniformed soldier.

Before going on to study later developments resulting from the words of the Proclamation, it is as well to pause at this point and consider one vitally important historical fact.

Over the years, fierce controversy has raged as to who exactly were the authors of the erudite and well-written Proclamation. Many felt it to be the composition of some of the Radical Leaders themselves. However, the Honorary President of the 1820 Society, Peter Berresford Ellis in the seminal study he co-authored with the late Seumas Mac A' Ghobhainn, 'THE SCOTTISH INSURRECTION OF 1820' (Gollancz,1970, and Pluto Free 1989) was of the considered opinion that the 'Rising' was really orchestrated behind the scenes by Government agent-provocateurs and by means of infiltrating spies into the Radical movement. As the 1820 Society in their latest Newsletter so rightly point out, "The aim was to lure the unsuspecting Radicals into taking premature 'action', allowing the authorities to respond with a vindictive programme of systematic suppression."

That they succeeded in this dastardly ploy is without doubt. From the 3rd April, 1820 and over the next few days, there were minor skirmishes, angry demonstrations and virtually complete work-stoppage throughout much of Scotland. And even although latterly, the streets of Glasgow were lined with troops, it was clear to anyone who stopped long enough to think about it, that the Military were acting under orders not to antagonise the populace, for fear of precipitating and causing another 'Peterloo' Massacre. Despite rumours, counter-rumours and much open marching and drilling in city streets, it was very soon clear that the main centre of rebel activity was in Paisley, with its hordes of militant weavers. The latter were obviously well-prepared for the envisaged fight. Not only had they woven on their own looms, cartridge webs which they supplied to the entire contingent of Paisley Radicals, they had even had printed their own Banknotes!

With these in readiness, for a Provisional Government, they were hoping to exchange them at some point for essential and possibly more sophisticated arms and ammunition. Meanwhile, they would make do with the homemade yet very efficient weapon known as the Radical cleg. This was a kind of dart made of lead and with a shuttlecock feature at the other end, to help speed it on its flight towards its intended victim.

While there was much activity behind the scenes in the making of weapons, plans were also afoot for greater Radical involvement on many issues of the day.

THE BATTLE of BONNYMUIR

What has come to be known as the Battle of Bonnymuir, in effect the Rising's major skirmish, took place on 5th April, 1820 near Falkirk. As the 1820 Society point out in their membership brochure the Battle came about as follows:

"The immediate military objective of the Rising was the capture of the armaments factory at the Carron Ironworks near Falkirk. The Radicals were however, intercepted by the British army at Bonnymuir and routed."

In their skirmish against members of the Yeomanry and the 10th Hussar regiment, Radical leaders John Baird of Condorrat, and Andrew Hardie of Glasgow were captured. Several of the luckier Radicals managed to escape custody. As for those severely wounded, these prisoners were helped into a cart by Baird and Hardie and made as comfortable as possible for the onward custodial journey to Stirling.

Once arrived at Stirling Castle, Fort-Major Peddie took charge of the prisoners and ordered that they be herded into a single cell. As for John Baird, who had been insisting that not only was he the sole leader, and he alone merited whatever punishment might be envisaged, he also made urgent appeals for his men, wounded, hungry and thirsty to be given food and water. For his pains, he was shortly conducted to a dungeon and unceremoniously clapped in irons, there to languish until his later execution.

As for the powers-that-be, the then Home Secretary, Lord Sidmouth was absolutely delighted with the outcome of the Battle, so much so that he went in person to see King George IV at Carlton House and deliver the 'glad tidings.'

There then followed great jubilation in England, Church bells were rung in honour of the event, mutual congratulations were the order of the day between the members of the ruling-class in both England and Scotland, there were even special editions - with biased, high-flown accounts - published of the 'LONDON GAZETTE.'

Yet all the while that the King and his Ministers were bent on self-congratulation, on the defeat of the Radical Army, things were anything but quiet on the Scottish scene.

In the days, weeks and months following the Battle of Bonnymuir, there were sporadic outbursts and many minor skirmishes between the Radicals and the forces of Law and Order. The most notable and decidedly the most violent of these was on 8th April, 1820 with the storming of Greenock Jail and the subsequent horrific massacre.

It was to be another three months or so of seething unrest throughout Scotland before the trials for High Treason started. And even throughout the duration of the Trials, there was much agitation, ill-feeling and confrontation in trouble-spots across Scotland. Any band caught playing 'SCOTS WHA HAE' was punished; committees were set up by employers with a view to banning from any future employment any and all known Radicals; military-style raids were conducted on various tenement dwellings, with a view to arresting known Radicals; and in some cases, Radicals who had been sacked from their jobs were accused, rightly or wrongly, of having led sporadic raids on the homes of their former employers.

And what ultimately became of the forty-seven Radicals who were captured at Bonnymuir and left thereafter to languish in gaol at Stirling?

Eventually, many of them had perforce to be released, after a number of somewhat farcical Trials in which Jurors throughout Scotland in general and Paisley in particular, were extremely reluctant to find the said prisoners guilty! Of those finally released, a number were transported and sent off in boats headed for Australia, New Zealand, and Canada.

But as far as the three leaders went, Baird, Hardie and James Wilson, the latter having been arrested at his own home in Strathaven, after being caught in a Government-spy trap, a very different fate awaited them... that of execution. And a public execution at that, cleverly stage-managed to serve as a warning to any Scots still harbouring notions of future Radical rebellion.

The first of the three men to be executed was James Wilson, an elderly weaver, who despite the appallingly slender grounds of his involvement, and in spite of massive public sympathy and even strong judicial recommendation for mercy, nevertheless received no last-minute reprieve. Right up till the last, it had been hoped that in common with another 19 condemned men, James Wilson's sentence also would be commuted to transportation for life to one of the far-flung Colonies of Great Britain. But it was not to be!

And on Wednesday 30th August, 1820 on a lovely summer's day, the gallows awaited James Wilson near the Justiciary Hall in Glasgow. It is worth noting that as a general rule, public executions of that period of history were generally conducive of something approaching a high day or holiday, with rumbustious spirits, laughter, and even hordes of stallholders doing brisk business in the sale of food, drink, gruesome souvenirs and other unconsidered trifles. But although on this historic occasion, the crowd had steadily grown to a massive 20,000 strong, by Noon of that day, there was still not a flicker of amusement, not a voice raised in anger, far less in drunken debauchery, and not even a single stallholder in sight!

Instead, there was a sullen, waiting, angry silence ... a truly menacing stillness, in which the only sound. to be heard was the rustle of illicit posters then being passed surreptitiously from hand to hand.

Little wonder then that the Army officer in charge of security, Major-General Reynell, felt it necessary to order reinforcements. And not just in the general area of the gallows, but throughout the streets of Glasgow, where he deployed members of the 3rd Dragoon Guards, 33rd Regiment of Foot and the 1st Battalion of the Rifle Brigade.

And it must be assumed that he felt every single recruited soldier be vital to the task of trying to keep order when he caught sight of the on the pamphlets and posters then being circulated through the ranks of

necessary to order reinforcements

the 'great un-washed.' This particular message was short and very much to the point...

"May the ghost of the butchered Wilson, haunt the pillows of his relentless jurors-
MURDER! MURDER! MURDER!"

The whole sorry business, the butchery of elderly weaver James Wilson began with -of all things - a religious service. Psalms were sung, in which the brave James Wilson joined, prayers were intoned and the Reverend Dr. Greville Ewing gave an impassioned address in which he assured the doomed man that "Who so calleth on the name of the Lord, calleth not in vain."

Even so, there was still to be no last-minute reprieve either heaven-sent or from his earthly captors. And so James Wilson was hanged, then some thirty minutes or so later, beheaded by the young man hired for the hideous task, one Thomas Moore, a 20 year-old student from Glasgow's Bridgegate.

The bloody job completed, the mangled body of martyr James Wilson was then bundled into a coffin which was then hastily and unceremoniously buried near Glasgow High Church in the 'Paupers' Ground.'

The relatives had been led to believe that the body, in accordance with James Wilson's own last wishes, would be given to them for decent Christian burial in Strathaven, his own home village and that of many other Radical weavers. Their pleas were ignored by those in authority and there the matter might have rested, had it not been for the persevering, daring and single-mindedness of purpose on the part of James Wilson's friends and relatives. The latter returned to the graveyard, where under the cover of darkness, at midnight they exhumed the body and wrapt the severed head in a white linen cloth for later decent burial in the Parish Churchyard of his native Strathaven. It is significant that while the powers-that-be were anything but pleased by this development, they subsequently took no official action against either the local Clergyman or any one of Wilson's relatives... no doubt they were by then terrified that punishment of the loyal perpetrators of this 'crime' would result not only in further uprising, but in nothing short of mob-rule.

On Friday September 8th, 1820, a similar fate awaited 28 year-old Andrew Hardie and 32 year-old John Baird. Yet again the same format was observed ... the scaffold erected, this time in Broad Street in front of Stirling Jail; the two rough coffins in readiness; the same young medical student once again dressed in the garb of executioner, with his face masked by a piece of black crepe. In this way died the other two martyrs of the Scottish Insurrection. Of those who were transported, nineteen Radicals took with them to Australia "the banner under which they had previously marched... 'SCOTLAND FREE or a DESERT.' The Insurrection was over but the high ideals would survive... 'SCOTLAND FREE OR A DESERT.'

MASSACRE at GREENOCK
The Scottish 'Peterloo'

In the days following the Battle of Bonnymuir and the subsequent Rising at Strathaven, the streets of Greenock - in stark contrast to those of Paisley and Glasgow - were relatively and surprisingly quiet ... at least as far as any additional Radical activity in the way of riots, demonstrations or protest marches were concerned.

However, down on the dockside, it was an entirely different matter. Here the quayside was black with a seething mass of humanity - former, fully-involved Radicals and their families, burdened with their unwieldy tied-up bundles of their meagre and pitiful possessions, and each man desperately seeking steerage passages aboard a waiting ship. Any ship would do, whether it was heading for America, Canada, Australia ... anywhere, as long as it would take them safely beyond the shores of their beloved Scotland, the long arm of the vengeful British army, and its rat-run of Government spies and 'agents provocateurs.'

At this time, such ships as the 'GEORGE CANNING', the 'DAVID', the 'CURLEW' and the appropriately-named, the 'BROKE' made regular voyages to the new world with their holds stuffed with human cargo. It must be said that living conditions on these over-crowded ships was hellish. All too often it was a case of packing in as many paying bodies into as little space as could physically be managed. Thus, with nothing other than profit in mind and scant or no regard for the safety, far less the comfort of steerage passengers, the holds would be fitted out with rough, double-tiered bunks. These were positioned as closely together as was humanly possible, with not a thought spared for any such niceties as statutory allowance as to permissible living-space.

Once the passengers were abed and the cargo hatches secured, the stench of unwashed bodies and vomit from sea-sickness can well be imagined. Such appalling conditions on the emigrant ships were a well-known fact of life. And yet, so desperate were these men, Radicals one and all, that they were prepared to endure such a voyage, in order to escape capture, lengthy imprisonment and perhaps even execution, should they remain a minute longer on their native soil.

Brave men that they were, they had done their best, their noble best in the glorious cause of Liberty for the downtrodden of their native Scotland. And to a man they knew in their hearts that in fleeing the Scottish shores, they would be carrying on the fight in another land, for they would be taking with them the dreams, the hopes and above all, their humanitarian ideals. For them, the fight would never be over. World history would in later years bear out the fact that these brave men and their equally courageous families, took their skills, their crafts and above all, their high ideals with them in good measure to their new homes far beyond auld Scotia's shores. What was in effect a dire loss to their native country, became the true grit of new, idealistic and eventually prosperous communities in many a far-flung outpost of the Empire.

But to return to the quiet, mean streets of Greenock in the year 1820. Away from the hustle of the dockside, the local people went about their normal business - unemployed men, aimless, and with the despair, the cancer of inactivity already gnawing at their very souls, hung about street-corners and waste-ground; their undernourished wives, old before their time with the double burden of childbearing and penny-pinching to feed their families and try to keep body and soul together, scavenged for scraps of food, all the while with the youngest bairn happed up in a moth-eaten shawl; and toddlers, nearly but not yet quite old enough to be employed as slave-labour in the mills, played in the filth and squalor of the gutter, with its stinking residue of puddles, assorted rubbish and the pungent odour of horse-dung.

That then was the scene when, in the weird way of such things, a strong rumour began to sweep through the town, the whispered news being passed from the lips of one citizen to the next. Eventually, such hurried and furtive whisperings became a gale of sound bearing along in its wake the thoughts, fears and hopes of the common people, the great 'un-washed'.

And what was this exciting news? Was it to be another battle? Were the people of Greenock now to be the ones to rise up in arms against their oppressors?

It would not have been surprising had that indeed been the case, considering the events of the past few days and the smug air of self-righteousness on behalf of their 'betters.' It had happened that on the Thursday of that week, with its being a religious Fast Day, churches in Glasgow and beyond were bursting at the seams with the well-clothed, decently-housed affluent merchant-class, who were there to give thanks to God for their safe and speedy deliverance from the rioting violence of the stinking, 'un-washed rabble.'

Even worse, many a pulpit rail that day was well and truly thumped in emphasis, as preachers declaimed against the Radicals, their dissolute followers and 'the great and bloody battle.' And God-fearing so-called Christians or not, and even though the general feeling was that the trouble of the Radical Insurrection and War was now safely behind them, nevertheless, members of the holier-than-thou ruling class, were hell-bent on revenge.

And it certainly did not take too academic a brain to realise that such revenge would take but one form ... that of a total ban on any question of re-employment of any and all known-Radicals who had taken an active part in the bloody uprising. In fact, close on fifty successful, highly prosperous Glasgow merchants went so far as to request the Hon. Henry Monteith, the then Lord Provost of Glasgow, to call a public meeting of the Merchants, Manufacturers, and Proprietors of Public Works 'for the purpose of considering what steps it may be proper to take regarding the future employment of those who have obeyed the command of a TREASONABLE CONFEDERACY to desist from their ordinary labour.'

Lord Provost Monteith was happy to agree to such a meeting, which he convened 'in the TOWN HALL on Tuesday, the 11th inst. at 12 o'clock noon.'

So, to return to that rumour then sweeping the mean, ill-lit streets, wynds and back-courts of Greenock ... what exactly was this mind-boggling news? It appeared that with the then overcrowding of Paisley Jail, Oliver Jamieson, the Lord Provost of Paisley, had called for troop re-inforcements to escort five 'prominent Radical leaders' through the town and onwards to Greenock, there to be lodged in the larger, more commodious Greenock Jail.

Colonel John Dunlop deputed Officer Carswell to prepare a

Company of thirty soldiers for the short journey. However, later on, he amended this to a Company 80-strong and an extra Officer, a man called Cleland. Colonel Dunlop took this step in view of the rumours which had reached his ears that there would be some Radical attempts to free the political prisoners, the very moment that they were clear of Paisley.

And leaving nothing to chance, Dunlop further intimated by letter sent via the driver of the Mail Coach to James Dennistoun, Chief Magistrate at Greenock, that the five prisoners, having been despatched in a cart at 12 Noon from Paisley, could be expected to arrive in Greenock some time in the late afternoon.

As is the way with verbally communicated rumours, by the time the news of the imminent arrival of the five prisoners had swept the town of Greenock, the expected number had grown, at least in the imagination of the local people, from the mere handful of five to a greatly exaggerated fifteen or sixteen!

Hardly surprising then that the waiting crowd had also grown in equal proportion. And by the time that Cleland and Carswell came riding along behind the drummers, they could not fail to notice that quite apart from the crowds of sullenly hostile people who stood around, on all sides every little shop was firmly closed and boarded-up, as though in readiness for who-knew-what violence to follow.

It was five o'clock on that Saturday night before the five political prisoners were safely lodged in the jail at Greenock. But even so, their escort, the Port Glasgow Militia, had had a hard fight to battle their way through the hostile crowds to reach the Bridewell.

It was when the troops started to march their way back again through the streets of Greenock that the real trouble erupted. At first the citizens of Greenock contented themselves with hurling verbal abuse, but on finding this to be of little avail, a few stalwarts then resorted to a spot of stone-throwing. This served only further to enrage the soldiers. In Cathcart Street, and opposite the Tontin Inn, the order was given by Carswell for a volley to be fired over the heads of the crowd. Far from obeying this command to the letter, the soldiers immediately opened fire indiscriminately. The end result of this bloody massacre was that nine people were killed, some dying instantly where they fell, and the others shortly afterwards in the local Infirmary. Of those killed, the youngest victim was 8 year-old James MacGilp, the others all youngish men in the prime of life, with 65 year-old John MacWhinnie being the oldest fatality.

In terms of carnage, horror and the appalling loss of innocent lives, not to mention the horrific injuries sustained by such people as 14 year-old Hugh Paterson and 65 year-old Mrs. Catherine Turner, both of whom later suffered the trauma and pain of leg amputation, the Greenock Massacre was in the same class as the world-renowned Peterloo Massacre. And yet, little or nothing is ever mentioned in the history books about this dark deed, nor even the fact that despite such carnage, such enormity of the deed, no disciplinary action was ever taken against the Port Glasgow Militia.

And even today, 176 years later, there is still, as the 1820 Society so rightly point out in their leaflet, 'no memorial, street-name or any commemoration whatsoever in Greenock to these working-class martyrs.'

In the wake of the massacre, the first instinct of the crowd, in a state of shock and stunned disbelief, was that they should head towards Port Glasgow, and there somehow avenge their innocent dead. However, realising that advance notice would already have been sent to Port Glasgow, they changed their tactics and instead decided to storm Greenock Jail. So it was that armed with stones, sticks, torn-up railings, and even in some cases with guns and swords, they finally managed to smash down the stout wooden gates of the prison.

That major obstacle removed, the angry crowd then stormed into the prison, where acting strictly by the book, they freed only the five political prisoners, and left severely alone those prisoners legitimately serving time for such crimes as theft, arson and rape.

By 10 o'clock on that Saturday night, the 8th April, 1820, quiet had again descended on the streets of Greenock ... but for many families who had lost their loved ones, life would never again be the same.

FOOTNOTE re EMIGRANT SHIPS SAILING FROM GREENOCK in 1820

One ship in particular which sailed from the West Quay, Greenock, in the year 1820 with a 'goodly number of emigrants for the Cape of Good Hope', was the good ship 'ABEONA'. An enterprising band of Scotsmen with their wives and families, they set out with hopes high, tools of their trade to hand, and their minds bent on "conquering a new home for themselves in South Africa", far from the troubles then besetting their own beloved Scotland.

But for this particular group of hopeful emigrants, Fate held a cruel trick in store...

It is thanks to the editor and reporters of the 'ROTHESAY EXPRESS' in commemorating, in 1885, the 65th anniversary of the sinking of the 'ABEONA' that we now have a complete record of events pertaining to the tragedy. Under the banner headline: 'A SAD STORY OF TRUE HEROISM', we learn that when sailing through the troubled waters of the Bay of Biscay, fire broke out on the ill-fated ship. "Their boats were few, all could not be saved and with sublime abnegation, the doomed emigrants filled the boats with their young children, and resigned themselves to death. 'Twas a terrible parting, but soon the 'ABEONA' and its noble men and women disappeared beneath the waves, while a cloud of steam floated heavenwards, fit incense of their dying prayers."

The now-orphaned children adrift in small boats, were lucky in that they were soon picked up by a passing Portuguese ship, whose crew cared for them until, on reaching Lisbon, they were sent onwards to Greenock, their original port of departure. There is a haunting similarity here between these returning shipwrecked children and those of 120 years later, the pathetic evacuee children from the 'CITY OF BENARES' who also returned to the port of Greenock.

One young survivor from the 'ABEONA', ten-year-old Mary in charge of two younger members of her family, together with a group of other orphans, remnant of the passengers who had left with such high hopes, was "marched up the old quay, with red nightcaps on their heads, and through some of the streets of the town to the old jail in Bank Street, where they found temporary lodgement till claimed by their friends."

As one can well imagine, there was scarcely a dry eye in Greenock on 'that memorable day.' Mary appears to have been the oldest member of the group, with at least three children from one family having been saved. Eventually, all the orphans were claimed by near-relatives and as for young Mary herself, she was taken to Glasgow where she was brought up by a couple of maiden aunts. It is interesting to note that until she reached the age of fourteen, Mary did not break the silence of depression which resulted from the horrific trauma of her experience. However, one evening while sitting before a fire, the subject of the sinking of the 'ABEONA' was mentioned, and Mary "startled her aunts by giving a full relation of the terrible event." It was to the following effect:

the fire had caught the sails

"I was wakened out of my sleep and hurriedly dressed by my mother, so were the younger children. Smoke was issuing from the fore-part of the ship and my little brother and sister were kissed by my father and mother, then passed to the sailors who handed them over the ship's side. I was then kissed, and told to be good, and to watch over my brother and sister, but I struggled and resisted with all my strength, and clung to my mother, but was also put into the boat. By this time, the fire had caught the sails, and the boat we were in was pushed off, and as we slowly drifted from the burning ship, I saw father and mother clasped in each other's arms, and gazing at our boat with looks that I'll remember to my dying day. All that night the ship was a pillar of fire on the Ocean, and I hid my face in my shawl from the sight, and at last fell asleep. When I awoke it was daylight, and a ship was close to the boats. We were taken on board, and you know the rest. And oh! Aunt! never more shall I tell the story of that awful night while I live, and never ask me to tell it again."

So there we have it, the full details of what befell the hopeful emigrants and Radicals who set sail from Greenock on board the 'ABEONA' in search of a new and hopefully better life. That they achieved neither, but only the hell of a watery grave is now history.

However, history does not record for us the names, hopes, and ambitions of those many other thousands of Scottish emigrants who, over time, drowned in the tempestuous waters of the world's Oceans. It is without doubt that there were indeed thousands of such poor souls when one considers that weekly statistics of shipwrecks was a normal feature of Scottish newspapers in the 1800's. To take but one example:

In the 'ROTHESAY EXPRESS' for December 26th, 1883, is the following summary:

"The shipwrecks reported last week numbered 56. Of these, 30 were British, and 26 foreign. In 7 cases, all on board perished, and in other 7 instances, there was loss of life. The total number of wrecks for the present year is now 1,914, as against 1,747 at the date last year."

One can only imagine that in 1820, given the even more primitive conditions then on board, the number of shipwrecks at least equalled, if not far exceeded the bald totals given for 1883.

Chilling statistics indeed when translated into the loss of dreams, ideals, and vibrant young lives, who had left the port of Greenock and their native Scotland with such high hopes of a better future - a future denied them by the cruel hand of Fate.

THE BLANTYRE CALAMITY

Death of 207 Miners

(First published in THE SCOTS MAGAZINE)

The 22nd October 1877 was a black day in the annals of Scottish history, for 207 hard-working young men were killed. It was not a ferocious battle which ended their lives, but the dangerous state of the mines in which they worked. Fire-damp had resulted in the disaster which came to be known as the Blantyre Calamity. Obviously, this loss of life was widely reported by the newspapers of the day, one of them *The Rothesay Express* of 24th October 1877:

At the time disaster struck there were 233 men and boys in the pits. The Upper Blantyre Colliery, the property of Messrs William Dixon & Company Limited, had always been noted for its freedom from foul air, and when the oversman went through the workings at six o'clock on Monday morning there was not the slightest indication of fire-damp.

Shortly before nine o'clock, however, the noise of a terrible explosion reached the mouth of No. 3 Pit, between which and No. 2 Pit there was the statutory communication of passages leading from one pit to another.

The certificated manager of the Blantyre Colliery was James Watson, then aged 37 and with 23 years experience of working in mines. He at once organised an exploring party and every exertion was made to obtain access to the colliers who, because of the damage done to the shafts by the explosion, were imprisoned in the workings. It was impossible to gain access by means of No. 3 Pit, as the volumes of choke damp - that clinging, noxious, carbonic acid gas which formed in mines after a fire-damp explosion - came rolling up the shaft and indicated only too well the stifling nature of the atmosphere below. The rescue party descended No. 2 Pit, and soon came upon several dead miners.

After 13 corpses had been taken to the surface, the explorers were forced back by the foul air, and were compelled to suspend all operations for some hours. While the rescue party was busy at No. 2 Pit, strenuous endeavours were made to clear the shaft of No. 3 Pit, and about three o'clock in the afternoon the workers, having reached within 25 fathoms of the bottom of the shaft, heard calls for help from the entombed colliers. The search continued during the greater part of Monday night, and again resumed the following morning. Only a few were taken out alive, and it was feared that more than 200 persons had died.

Dr William Grant tended the injured when they were taken to the engine house, where he washed and dressed their wounds. Yet despite his valiant efforts, most of the injured miners were too far gone to survive, for in addition to their horrific burns, they had swallowed a considerable amount of black or choke-damp.

One man who had a miraculous escape from the sudden death which was the fate of so many of his fellow-miners was Alexander McCall, firemaster at No. 3 Pit. He later described his experiences in *the Hamilton Advertiser*:

"I descended into the pit at a quarter past four o'clock in the morning along with John Laidlaw and an underground manager, John Pickering. He explored the whole of the workings thoroughly and found them all right, and the ventilation free. The men commenced to come down the pit at half past five in the morning, and all were down a few minutes past six o'clock. The total number, according to the justiceman at the pit-head, including ourselves, being 107. The men commenced to work as usual about half past eight, or between that and twenty minutes to nine. We left the levels and came to the pit-mouth for the purpose of ascending the shaft, in order to take breakfast. We reached the pit-head, when at ten minutes to nine o'clock we were put into terrible confusion. At that time there were about 20 men at the pit-head, some drawing the hutches from there to the waggon coups, and others attending to the various duties which they find at the pit-head. Suddenly, we were startled by a report like the firing of many cannons, but louder than the loudest thunder I ever heard."

This was followed by dense volumes of smoke ascending the shaft, then a vast sheet of flame rolled up from the pit with a hissing noise, followed by showers of wood, dirt and stones. Among the debris was the mangled limb of an unfortunate youngster. This eruption lasted from four to five minutes. Then all fell eerily quiet. Many of those at the pit-head had their whiskers, eyebrows and hair singed; Mr Watson, the manager had his face and hands scorched.

Alexander McCall and his companions were momentarily dumbstruck. Then they ran to No. 2 Pit to see what could be done, but found the connection stopped, although some men were rescued. Then they came back to No. 3 Pit, unhooked the cage from the tow-rope, and put on the "kettle", a barrel-like vehicle used mainly in sinking pits. Because of its shape, the kettle could pass up or down a shaft where a cage could not go.

Many men were anxious to descend to the pit and explore, to save more colleagues and friends and also to learn the true state of affairs. John Pickering, a Cornishman named Coulter, and McCall got into the kettle and were lowered. They reached 180 feet, where they found the shaft hopelessly blocked by debris. They were compelled to ascend to the surface to get materials for repair work.

At the hour of the explosion, according to the figures given at the Pay Office, it would appear that 126 men were then working down in No. 2 Pit, with 107 in No. 3, thus making a total of 233 miners, but it would seem that the actual number was in excess of this. For some reason the fire-damp, as well as the flame, was more severe on the south side than it was on the north. Consequently nearly all the men employed in the latter working escaped to the pit-mouth, and were drawn to the top. However, not a single miner in the south side of the pit managed to escape.

Another eye-witness said: "The explosion was like the bursting of a boiler, or a salvo of artillery, succeeded by a rumbling noise like that of distant thunder."

The dull, rumbling sound heard above ground indicated at once that something was wrong. Then a tremendous volume of flame was vomited forth from No. 3 shaft, smashing completely the cage and the woodwork, and injuring severely Mr Watson, the manager, and some joiners making repairs about the mouth of the pit.

Two of these men, it is said, were blown a distance of 20 feet, but this conveys only a faint idea of the violence of the explosion, for it must be remembered that the flame - if the previously-given locality of the explosion is correct - must have travelled over 2800 feet before finding the mouth of No. 3 shaft. After this volume of fire, said to have carried with it a quantity of coal dust that darkened the air, there came a rumbling noise in the shaft. This indicated only too plainly that the bratticing, a partition in coal-mines for ventilation, had been damaged and that a portion of the sides had fallen in. When the results of the disaster came to be examined, it was impossible to reach the bottom of No. 3 Pit as the wall between had been partially blown down.

At No. 2 shaft less damage resulted, because fire-damp explosions always travel against the current of air. So a few minutes after the accident, a number of men who had been working at the north face were brought safely to the surface.

As soon as the news of the disaster became known, miners from all the surrounding pits gathered together, determined to try to rescue their surviving comrades. Such was the intensity of feeling at what had happened that no fewer than 2000 miners from the neighbouring pits marched along the road towards Blantyre, determined to descend the ill-fated mine en masse. At the same time, Alexander McDonald, MP, having heard of the calamity, was also rushing to High Blantyre. Seeing this mass of humanity on the march, he at once stopped to address the men and point out to them the folly of endangering even more lives. His impassioned plea finally convinced the miners who, albeit reluctantly, were dissuaded from their act of bravery. Even so, the very fact of their spontaneous attempted action to help the already-doomed miners, shows not only the empathy for their fellow-workers, but also their unflinching bravery.

Another assembly of heartbroken people could be seen wending their weary way to the pit-head. Streams of women and children were issuing from the rows of houses adjacent to the colliery, while from High Blantyre and farther away, groups of men and women of all ages, many still scantily attired and all with fearful expressions, came hurrying towards the pits. According to their knowledge of the whereabouts of friends and relations, they made their way to No. 2 or No. 3 Pit, surrounded the shafts, and enquired after fathers and brothers, sons and husbands. Piercing shrieks were heard of: "Oh, my puir faither, let me hae my faither!" "My man, my bonnie man, bring him to me!" "My dear wee laddies, what am I tae dae withoot them?"

All with fearful expressions came hurrying towards the pits

Strong men shed tears or wrung their hands in silent agony. One man who overheard the question, "How did it happen?" said, "I ken, I ken; I've two boys in the pit; it was the takin doon o the stoops." The stoops referred to massive pillars of coal, left to support the roof. At the subsequent official inquiry, it emerged that over two months earlier than the Blantyre Calamity itself, an explosion of fire-damp had given warning of the condition of the mine; in that particular incident Joseph McAnulty, who had a contract for working out the stoops, was severely burned and died from his injuries.

As gradually the maimed and bloodied corpses were brought to the pit-head, they were covered by a coarse blanket for decency's sake and conveyed to the wright's shop which had been converted into a morgue. After identification - when it was possible to identify the remains - the bodies were taken to a shed, a short distance away. Even now, 115 years later, we can still imagine the anguish of the bereaved. On hand throughout the ordeal to give them spiritual comfort were the parish minister, the Reverend Stewart Wright and his assistant, who tended to the welfare of the sufferers connected with the Established Church; the Reverend Father Frawley to those of the Roman Catholic persuasion; and the Reverend Mr McDonald for Free Church members.

Queen Victoria sent, on the Wednesday of the week of the disaster, the following telegram:

"The Queen wishes to know the extent of the sad disaster in the colliery, and hopes it may not be so great as reported."

A further message from the Secretary of State to Messrs Moore and Willis, Her Majesty's Inspectors of Mines, in the form of a telegram pointed out:

"The Secretary of State has directed that a public inquiry into the cause of the Blantyre Colliery accident shall be held by Mr Dickinson (one of Her Majesty's Inspectors of Mines) and a legal assessor. Please make this known." The Inspectors at once acknowledged receipt of this message and caused a copy of the telegram to be posted at the colliery.

As to the actual burial of the bodies, the melancholy scene was witnessed on Wednesday 31st October 1877 in the village burying-ground. When it was realised that such a large number of men had perished, the proprietors of the colliery secured the north-eastern portion of the new burial ground. Two trenches, upwards of 50 yards long, about three yards wide and two yards deep, were prepared. It was not intended to pile the coffins one above another, as was sometimes done in such cases, but to pack them closely together side by side.

Down the street leading to the cemetery, a mournful procession passed about three o'clock. The lines of people on the pavement consisted mainly of women who wept bitterly, wringing their hands.

The first of the victims to be buried was William Campbell, Smith's Lane, Kirkton. When his father, an elderly man, was leaving the ground, he suddenly became ill, and was able to proceed home only with the assistance of some friends. The next was Nicholas Kyle, Schoolhouse Lane, High Blantyre. The usual services were conducted in the houses of both bereaved families by the Rev. Riddell, Glasgow, Superintendent of the United Presbyterian Mission.

On the following day, Thursday 1st November, a large cortege of Roman Catholic victims left for Dalbeth Cemetery, where later a monument was erected to the memory of those who died.

As with all such disasters, there were tales of many who, by some quirk of fate, had somehow managed to evade death underground. There were also men who, for one reason or another, had not gone down the pit that particular day. Less fortunate, however, was 20-year-old Thomas Halliday who five or six months previously had left his job as a miner and enlisted with the 26th Cameronians, proceeding to Paisley to join the regiment. Prior to the departure of the corps to the south, Halliday was allowed a leave of absence for six weeks, time he resolved to spend with his friends. On Monday he volunteered to join his father in No. 2 Pit, in order to contribute to his earnings, but along with his father and a half-brother, Thomas became a victim. A sad irony indeed!

The history of coal-miners in Scotland is not a happy one. Even in Victorian days and at the time of the Blantyre Calamity itself, it was a fact of life that miners, and their overworked, downtrodden wives and children, were regarded as not only the lowest of the low, but as almost a race apart from their more fortunate fellow-Scots. In their squalid hovels - which no amount of cleaning and scrubbing could make habitable, far less comfortable - they knew themselves to be ignored, virtually abandoned and of no great concern to those in high office. It was only at times of such appalling disasters as the Blantyre Calamity that anyone took the slightest heed of their plight. How else could it have come about that even on the Sabbath, the most holy of days, miners and their families were frequently kept apart from other members of the congregation! To achieve this distinctly non-Christian goal, specially-built galleries with exterior staircases were constructed - e.g. the one at Newton Parish Kirk.

The harshness of life for mining families was further demonstrated in *the Hamilton Advertiser* of 18th May 1878. It was reported that Sheriff Birnie had before him 34 summonses of ejectment at the instance of William Dixon Ltd., against widows whose husbands were killed at High Blantyre Collieries on 22nd October 1877. Widow after widow pleaded the same reason for not removing - that of not getting enough money from the Relief Fund with which to keep their families and pay a rent. One widow said that the firm should have ejected her on the day of the explosion, as the public would then have taken her by the hand. Despite such pleas, Sheriff Birnie decreed that "both the Messrs Dixon and the public have been extremely kind and generous." Thus, except where illness was involved, removal was decreed for 28th May, the Term-day at Blantyre. It was also reported that "the proceedings were of a painful character."

The Coal Mines Regulation Act of 1872 was supposed to make mine-owners more responsible, and also render the mines safer. The

Blantyre Calamity made it painfully obvious that this had not happened. Even worse perhaps, was that two years later, on 9th July 1879, newspapers of the time carried yet another banner headline:

ANOTHER DREADFUL COLLIERY EXPLOSION AT BLANTYRE

"An explosion occurred on Wednesday night about 10 o'clock in No. 1 Pit, High Blantyre, of which Messrs W. Dixon and Co. Limited are the proprietors. Of the 31 brushers engaged in the ell seam, 27 have been killed and four badly injured. Twenty-three bodies were recovered on Thursday, but four still remain in the pit. To reach these, the efforts of the exploring party are directed. A large number of miners employed in another part of the pit were unaffected by the blast and escaped. Several of the exploring party nearly succumbed to the noxious gas and had to be conveyed to the surface. The pit communicates with No. 3 and may be said to be part of the same mine. The disaster is all the more startling that an explosion took place in this mine on 22nd October 1877, when 207 lives were lost."

Is it any wonder that people felt revulsion and waves of shock, anger and disbelief? We might wonder what lessons, if any, had been learned from the original Blantyre Calamity and to what extent the provisions of the 1872 Mines Act had been enforced.

All the more reason then, to commemorate and honour the dead of Upper Blantyre on 22nd October 1992, the 115th anniversary of the Blantyre Calamity.

A TRAGIC HOGMANAY

Disaster in a Paisley Cinema

Traditionally, Hogmanay in Scotland is a time of happy anticipation. It is also the last day of the year on which house-proud Scottish wives and mothers clean, polish, and scrub to within an inch of life anything or anybody who stands still long enough to be thus dusted, re-arranged or otherwise scourged of the year's dirt.

What better time then for Scottish weans, still on holiday from school, and dreading the annual clean-up, to flee to the anonymity, the comfort, the enjoyment of Hollywood escapism in the dark of the local flea-pit? Also, in this way, they could make an early start on celebrating the New Year.

If truth be told, many Scottish families would be glad to 'see the back' of 1929. The year had started badly with a virulent Influenza epidemic which had raged through the country and had left many families decimated, a trail of misery in its wake, and in many areas, school attendances down to an all-time low of 49%. Then too, there had been the added misery, the cancer of unemployment spreading its insidious tentacles across the face of Scotland. In a desperate bid to get work, there had been an influx of the unemployed into such towns and Cities as Paisley, Glasgow, Dundee. So, any family which had somehow survived to the year's end, was in a mood to celebrate the Hogmanay of 1929 ... it would be a case of 'guid riddance tae the auld' and then let's hurry on into, not only the New Year, but also the New Decade, with hopefully, brighter prospects.

So, in such a spirit of renewed hope, why not splurge out, for once, the carefully-hoarded bawbees and give the weans their tuppence each entrance-fee required for an afternoon at the local Picture Palace?

Thus, in the mood of the time, in picture-houses throughout the country on that Tuesday, 31st December, 1929, there were special matinée performances; and not least in Paisley, where, at the 'GLEN Cinema', there was, enticingly, a double-feature programme on offer.

The 'GLEN Cinema' was unusual in that far from being the usual plush, well-upholstered Picture Palace, it had started life as a Hall, a functional, largely comfortless meeting-place for the *Independent Order of Good Templars*.

So it was that the seating accommodation consisted of nothing other than bare wooden planks, without even the added comfort of a single arm-rest at the end of the bench. But as far as profit-margins went, this meant that a greater number of small children could be packed, like sardines, on to each wooden bench. Given the normal high spirits of children at any given time of unsupervised behaviour, far less at Hogmanay with all its many excitements, treats and promises of better things to come, then one can easily imagine the larking-about on those stark wooden benches. Any small, shy, or otherwise timid child would soon have been pushed off the end of the bench with the greatest of ease by the combined physical strength and cunning of those bullies, more surely and safely ensconced in the middle of the seating.

In the light of what later happened, it was reported that upwards of 700 children attended that fatal matinée on the very last day of the 1920's decade. This in itself would appear to be a very considerable number. However, given the fact of toddlers sitting on the knees of big sisters, in whose care they had been placed, and even babes-in-arms, then the number may indeed have well exceeded the earlier figure quoted. In fact, recent research for this book has turned up a cold and chilling statistic which states that "2,000 were watching a special Hogmanay Film Show."

Whatever the exact number, and it would appear to be somewhere between the two stated figures, the fact remains that the Hall was packed to suffocation - and the word is used advisedly!

In the normal way, the ground-floor of the 64'x43' Hall was officially recognised as providing seating for 612 adults. When one considers that not only was the ground-floor packed with shoulder-to-shoulder children, but also every available aisle and gangway, to say nothing of those youngsters hiding illegally in the forbidden balcony area, then the word 'overcrowded' hardly does justice to this seething maelstrom of highly-excited children.

Of the adults inside the 'GLEN Cinema' on that winter's afternoon, they were but six in number, namely the Manager; the Film

Operator, a man called Alexander Rosie; his Assistant, himself but a young lad of 15 years; one woman at the entrance pay-box; a girl selling sweets and chocolate; and a solitary attendant.

So, what exactly happened in the dark of the 'GLEN Cinema' on that fateful afternoon? It was a double-feature on offer that day and with the first reel of 'DESPERADO DUDE' already having been shown, as was normal practice, the young assistant took the finished reel along to the rewinding room.

Having duly re-wound the film and secured it in its tin container, the young lad placed it on top of a nearby electrical accumulator. This latter six-volt machine was used to provide power for the Cinema's panatrope, a musical instrument of the time which was a well-advertised and highly entertaining special feature of the 'GLEN' and one of which the Cinema was justly proud.

About to get another reel out of its box, the Assistant-Projectionist was startled to hear a strange 'whooshing' sound. Thinking that it indicated a gas-leak of some kind, he immediately went out to the corridor, there to check up on a radiator. Finding that all was well, he at once returned to the rewinding room to continue with his duties. Imagine his consternation when he was met at the door by clouds of smoke issuing from the container on top of the accumulator. At once alert, and sensing the very real danger of fire raging through the rewinding room with its highly inflammable stocks of film, he grabbed hold of the smoking canister and darted at high speed for the nearest exit.

Had he been able, as was his intention, to toss the smoking tin out on to the waste-ground which he knew lay beyond at the foot of the steps, then all would have been well.

But Fate decreed otherwise - the door resisted all his frantic efforts to open it. What to do now? One can imagine the panic building up within the fifteen-year-old boy, so frighteningly alone with the smoking canister, and his the decision as to what to do for the best.

Wisely deciding that help would be needed in trying to force open the door, he left the smoking tin and at once reported to his immediate superior, Alexander Rosie, the Film Projectionist, who in turn despatched him to seek out the Manager.

In order to reach the Manager's Office, the by-now panic-stricken lad had first to battle his way along a gangway - and as we have already noted, these were already chockablock with children whose ages ranged from toddlers to 14-year-olds. Desperation and the thought of the still-smouldering can, lent him the physical and moral strength to wade through the human wall with little ceremony, so that after a deal of pushing and shoving, he did at last reach the Manager's Office, was able to gasp out his story and immediately recruit the help of the older man.

However, the pair still had to make the return journey along the child-packed aisle and through the crowded auditorium, with all the while, as they knew only too well, there were precious minutes ticking by.

Once safely back in the now smoke-filled rewinding room, they removed the flat-topped canister, and then with their combined strength managed to force open the door. That done, the Manager gave a hefty kick to it, and the smoking canister with its poisonous fumes still spewing forth, went spinning off down the steps and towards the waste-ground. One can well imagine the sighs of relief from the Manager and his young Assistant-Projectionist, for apart from the clouds of smoke still hanging about the rewinding room and the corridor, the immediate danger was clearly past. The Manager must have felt happy that having done his best to avert a fire tragedy, the crowded Cinema and its boisterous matinée patrons were safe. Yes! Fate was finally on his side ... or was it?

Meanwhile, in the unsupervised Auditorium, the children totally unaware of either the existence of the smouldering canister or the vitally important fact of its having been ejected from the building, were nevertheless beginning to panic!

All that the children were aware of was the fact of huge clouds of smoke suddenly belching into the hall. That, together with the previous unprecedented dash through the auditorium of the Manager, in their young eyes, a figure of authority and respectability, and as such, an august personage not normally given to running about in such an abandoned fashion, was enough to convince them of danger. As with one mind, they decided that they were in immediate and very real danger of being trapped in a fire.

It took only a few voices raised in calling "FIRE! FIRE!" for the panic, the stampede, the rush to escape to get under way. The tragic irony is that by this point in time, such a panic-driven exodus was entirely unnecessary, for any danger there had been, any threat of fire, was now well and truly over.

Even at this late stage, all might still have been well, especially when children at the front of the stampede managed, unaided, to operate successfully the push-bar mechanism on the Exit doors. But a cruel Fate was against them in the form of a securely-locked steel-gate, which thus effectively barred their way to safety and the nearby escape-route of the riverside path. There was no way forward and with the press of bodies then behind them, there was quite decidedly to be no way back. In short, their hellish Fate was sealed.

The film, till that point, still showing up on the screen, then finally ground to a halt. This was the final straw, the signal for all hell to break loose within the overcrowded auditorium, as hundreds of children, in frantically attempting to flee a threat which had no reality, instead met a hideous death, the very idea of which hardly bears thinking about.

When rescue teams of Police, Firemen and civilian volunteers effected entry in to the 'GLEN Cinema', they were faced with a grim sight - on a packed stairway, a mere ten steps from safety, lay waist-high piles of the dead and dying children; atop one mass of crushed bodies lay a pitiful 18-month-old baby; while still others were huddled together, either under benches or in the orchestra-pit; some boys and girls, in a blind panic had obviously tried to climb up the very screen itself, only to fall and lie in a heap at the foot of the silver screen; and behind the curtains up on the stage and clasped in each other's arms, were sisters who had died together.

So great had been the chaos at the height of the panic that several of the gas-light fittings had been badly damaged and it is thought that some of the young victims may have been poisoned and struck down by the resulting lethal gas-fumes.

In the streets outside the Cinema and all around Paisley Cross, there were frantic scenes as volunteers carried casualties out to waiting tramcars for the onward journey to the nearest Hospital; and anxious parents and relatives, half-demented by worry, strained to catch a glimpse or hear any scrap of news relating to possible family survivors.

The end result of the tragedy was that 70 children died, either crushed and trampled to death; suffocated from the weight of bodies; or poisoned by gas-fumes; several families each lost two children in the disaster, with at least one devastated family losing the grim total of three children.

In the aftermath of the tragedy, photographs taken of the 'GLEN Cinema' showed piles of abandoned scarves, sweetie-bags, half-eaten oranges and school trench-coats, together with an assortment of gloves, berets and bunnets.

And still on the outside of the 'GLEN' building was the hoarding announcing the second-feature film which had been programmed to follow the screening of the 'DESPERADO DUDE'. It is indeed ironic and a cruel twist of Fate, that the other film billed was entitled 'The CROWD.'

Further research for this book has shown that 'The CROWD', featuring Eleanor Boardman and James Murray as the stars, was advertised as: "A powerful and fascinating drama of a man and woman's fight to rise above the throng ... to get out of the rut and win the right to live."

Such children as Ina Peacock, a promising young Highland Dancer with prize medals to her credit; and Francis Curran, the son of Rothesay parents who had earlier moved to Paisley where job prospects were then marginally better than on the Island of Bute .... such victims were certainly not able to 'rise above the throng'. Nor did they 'win the right to live.' Instead, a cruel Fate decreed that with adulthood denied them, they were interred in a mass burial at Hawkhead Cemetery.

Hogmanay, that last Hogmanay of the 1920's decade was for the town of Paisley, the City of Glasgow and indeed the entire country of Scotland a black day, and one which should not be either forgotten or omitted from the pages of Scotland's past.

WILLIAM ALEXANDER SMITH
Founder of the Boys' Brigade

The Boys' Brigade, the world's oldest uniformed youth Organisation was founded by a Scotsman, William Alexander Smith.

Who was William Smith? What prompted him to become engaged in youth work? And what significance worldwide did this first-ever uniformed youth organisation have on later such developments?

William Alexander Smith was born on 27th October 1854 at Pennyland House on the outskirts of Thurso in Caithness. Even as a ten-year-old boy, William Smith was wont to form his school friends into a ragged squad and at every opportunity, spend many a happy hour drilling them. It is strange to think that from such a small beginning evolved a famous youth movement whose influence and rôle model eventually spread throughout the world.

When his father died in 1868, the 14-year old William and his mother had, by force of circumstance, to leave Thurso and the life they knew and loved there in the far north of Scotland, and instead, re-locate in the then unknown quantity of the City of Glasgow.

They settled in the Hillhead area, and soon William joined his uncle in attending the College Free Church in Lynedoch Street. This prosperous Church had a continuous programme of City Mission work, especially in the burgeoning new district of North Woodside in Glasgow's West End. By the time he was twenty and fully employed in his uncle's export business, William Smith was already devoting weekends, holidays and in fact, all his spare time to conducting Bible study groups and Sunday School classes.

In 1874 the American evangelists Moody and Sankey held a very successful Scottish campaign, in the course of which they advocated even greater social awareness and positive action to help the deprived of the Second City of the Empire.

At this point in its history, the College Free Church had a dedicated young Minister, the Reverend George Reith, who, like his parishioner William Smith, was deeply impressed by Moody's message of greater humanity and compassion to be shown to the poor of the City.

What particularly exercised William Smith's mind, as he sought to alleviate the poverty, privation and hardship he saw on all sides, was the uncertainty of the fate which awaited the 14 year old lads of his Sunday School classes ..... boys who, the moment they started work in foundry, factory or coal-mine, at once deemed themselves too old for such childish pursuits as attendance at Sunday school.

Coming as he did from a military family, William Smith was convinced that discipline of some sort was essential as an aid to training these young Scottish lads in the way they should go in order to become good and responsible citizens. But how was this desirable concept to be enforced?

After much thought and a great deal of heart-searching, William Smith came up with the idea of forming these impressionable lads into a group of some sort. Further to that, he became convinced that if, apart from discipline, he were to offer them a smart uniform, comradeship, drill, sport and military methods, then the interest of his former Bible-study and Sunday School students would be retained.

Once the somewhat revolutionary concept was clear in his own mind, William Smith spent the Spring and Summer of 1883 in discussing his ideas with colleagues at the North Woodside Mission. He met with some doubt and later on a measure of opposition from the officials and office-bearers of the College Free Church. However, with some backup from such Mission colleagues as James Moffat and James and John Hill, he finally won the day.

So it was that on October 4th 1883, in the West End of Glasgow, the inaugural meeting of the world's first-ever uniformed youth organisation was held.

Over time, lads who came along to meetings managed to scrape up enough money to buy their hats, haversacks and belts.

The weekly meeting fast became an enjoyable and important part of life for those Glasgow lads who had quickly flocked to join, once the news of this innovative group reached their ears.

One major and highly-sought-after activity was the formation of a Company band, and the prospect of learning to play the bugle, flute or drums was, of course, an added incentive and as, over time, the boys further developed their hitherto unsuspected musical talents, they were awarded the appropriate proficiency badges.

However, as far as the marching band was concerned, in the early days, all was not sweetness and light. And on many a Sunday morning, the parade of boys in their little round hats, dark suits, belts around their waists, haversacks slung over their chests, met with torrents of abuse in the city streets. Even worse, ragged urchins slouching on street corners threw rotten fruit, stones, rubbish -- in fact, anything on which they could lay their hands -- at the smartly-turned-out members of the Boys' Brigade marching bands.

Unruffled by such moronic behaviour, the boys of the B.B. went on their way through the Sabbath streets, marching their way into history.

Within a few years, the concept, activities and ideals of the B.B. movement had spread to all major cities throughout Britain. And with its motto of 'SURE AND STEDFAST' (keeping to the biblical spelling of 'Steadfast'), the B.B., with its comprehensive range of activities, added a whole new dimension to the lives of many hundreds of thousands of young men and boys.

In addition to indoor games and semi-educational topics conducted in the B.B. 'Club Rooms', the movement also pioneered camping. In 1886, the inaugural organised camp was held at Tighnabruaich in the Kyles of Bute, with the 1st Glasgow Company.

Gradually the B.B. movement gathered in popularity and momentum until it had spread worldwide to over 60 countries. Not only that, but it attracted strong support from many quarters and not least in a steady stream of interested and highly-qualified instructors. One such was Lord Baden-Powell, from whose involvement later developed the Boy Scouts movement. Many other official groups for boys -- the Church Lads' Brigades; the Boy's Life-Brigade, and even the Girls' Guildry, all these and more followed in the wake of the pioneer work instigated by William Smith.

For his achievements and his services to youth, William Alexander Smith was knighted in 1909 by Edward VII.

When William Smith died in 1914, Lord Baden-Powell in paying tribute to this far-seeing Scotsman, said of him:

"To other movements coming after his, the work is light. His was the groping through the dark tangle -- always looking to a light ahead -- his was the inspiration which has brought men and movements speeding after him."

And even thirty years after his death, his work was still being praised when King George VI at an Anniversary Parade, summed up the career of the remarkable William Smith of Thurso with the words:

"Your Founder builded better than he knew, for he started not only a great movement but one from which all our widespread youth training was to spring."

Stirring words indeed, and words which should be recalled with pride when we think of William Alexander Smith, a visionary from the far north of Scotland. He was a man who changed for the better the lives and prospects of thousands of young people..... young lads and lassies who until then had lacked a sense of purpose, achievement, and comradeship.

Scottish Men

Andrew Anderson

The Champion Draughts-Player of Scotland

On the first day of March, 1996, it was the 135th anniversary of the death of one of Scotland's famous sons, ANDREW ANDERSON.

Never heard of him? That is hardly to be wondered at, since although well-known and highly respected in his own lifetime, in his native Scotland and also across the Atlantic, in both Canada and America, the achievements and claim to fame of Andrew Anderson, have now, sadly, been lost in the mists of Time.

Like so many successful men and women from Scotland's past, young Andrew was born to poverty and brought up in a family which although lacking in material goods, nevertheless wanted for nothing in the way of a guid carin', lovin' and religious upbringing in the tried and tested Scottish tradition. And in addition to being trained in the right way as to the understanding and adoption of proper moral values, the boy was doubtless encouraged to develop and win 'a guid conceit o' hissell.'

There would, of course, have been little or no money available for such delicacies as 'snasters' or other sweet-bites. Even so, young Andrew would have been reared to manhood on a healthy diet of parridge, pease-brose, bannocks, tatties, herrin', mealie-puddens, and the good old stand-by - nourishing and mouth-watering Scotch Broth.

His childhood and a brief spell of education under the eagle eye of the local Dominie, soon over, Andrew was apprenticed to a weaver. An apt and willing pupil, he quickly mastered the intricacies of the craft, and over time, he became a stocking-weaver to trade. He is known to have continued to ply his trade until just shortly before his death in 1861.

However, the reader will already have surmised that this was not his claim to fame.

Like many another before and since, he had a lifelong interest, a hobby, which being entirely outwith the confines of his humdrum daily life, provided an escape route for his otherwise non-extended, but obviously razor-sharp, mental abilities.

But what made weaver Andrew different from others of his day was that not only did he enjoy his hobby of Draughts-playing, he went on to become an expert in this field. Yes! in due course, he evolved as a world authority on the subject.

The game of Draughts is known and played throughout the world. There is hardly a home in the land which has not at some time or another boasted a set, and many a wet afternoon or cold winter's evening around a coal-fire has been spent in playing endless bouts of this enjoyable and harmless game. In fact, even the very mention of the name 'Draughts', at once conjures up a mental picture of the board, its black and white 'men', and many an enjoyable family 'battle' over the result. Scottish Memories indeed!

Known as *Checkers* in America, Draughts is one of the oldest games in the world, a version of it having been played in the days of the early Egyptian Pharaohs, somewhere in or around the year 1600 B.C. And even more amazing, perhaps, it was mentioned in the works of the Greek writers, Plato and Homer.

But it was a Scotsman who actually went to the trouble of setting down the exact rules of the game. Yes! You've guessed it ... none other than our friend and lowly-born Andrew Anderson.

His definitive book: 'THE GAME OF DRAUGHTS- Simplified and Illustrated with Practical Diagrams' was published in Lanark in 1848.

This scholarly work, quickly regarded as the authority on the subject, was so popular that a second edition appeared in 1852, this time published in Glasgow. Then in 1878, no less than 17 years after the death of its author, 'THE GAME OF DRAUGHTS' went into a third edition. Another author, and obviously aficionado of the centuries-old game, revised and extended Andrew's original manuscript. That done, Robert McCulloch (from his name, another Scot, perhaps?) saw the latest edition published in both Glasgow and, across the Atlantic, in New York.

Altogether, 'no bad gaun' for a humble weaver who lived out his otherwise uneventful life in and around Carluke, Lanarkshire, and died at Braidwood, near Carluke on 1st March, 1861.

But even his book was not the full extent of his fame with regard to the game of Draughts. Thanks entirely to many years of devoted and intense practice, ANDREW ANDERSON became thoroughly skilled at the game. And to such good effect that in time he evolved as 'The Champion Draughts-player of Scotland.' This event, together with details of his definitive work, is given full credence and importance in an entry in no less a prestigious publication than 'The Dictionary of National Biography.'

Altogether, no' a bad record for a lowly member of what Scottish historians used to refer to as 'Lads o' Pregnant Pairts.'

Andrew Anderson became thoroughly skilled at the game

GEORGE SKENE KEITH
The 'Starving Doctor' of Edinburgh

Long known as a nation of intrepid colonisers, we Scots have also, over time, proved ourselves to be innovators in every field and in every corner of the globe.

In this book, it is hoped to take a detailed look at some of the men and women, often from very humble walks of life, who helped to make the name of Scotland famous throughout the world.

As is already well-known, nowadays many people are deeply into 'healthy' eating, the holistic approach and various forms of alternative medicine. Perhaps not quite such common knowledge is the indisputable fact that not only has it all been done before, but it was a far-seeing Scot who was the main pioneer in this field.

In January 1996, it was exactly 99 years since Doctor George Skene Keith, from his home in Currie, Midlothian, sat writing the preface to his book *Fads of an Old Physician*. He came by this particular title since he was fully aware that throughout his life, 'most of my peculiar ideas have been looked on and spoken of as "Fads" by my medical friends.' From this it will be at once apparent that his firmly held but in-advance-of-their-time ideas were ridiculed and held up to scorn by other doctors of the day. Not only were his theories reviled, but he himself earned the nickname of "The Starving Doctor of Edinburgh."

However, despite such opposition and ridicule, Dr. Keith held firmly to his beliefs to the end of his long life. He was of the opinion that 'the faddist not infrequently gains the day in the long run.' And so, in a spirit of hope for the future, he adopted the word 'Fads' in the title of his thought-provoking and highly controversial book.

Who exactly was this doctor who stirred up such heated arguments among other members of the medical profession? What was his background? And, finally, did he himself experiment to the point of using his controversial ideas with regard to his own health and well-being?

George Skene Keith, born at the Manse of St. Cyrus, Kincardineshire, a son of the then well-known 'Keith of the Evidences', started on his distinguished career in 1836. In that year he entered Edinburgh University and later had the distinction of being first Gold Medalist in the class of Professor James Young Simpson, the discoverer of the anaesthetic virtues of chloroform. One of the last of the Edinburgh 'apprentices', Dr. Keith later often spoke highly of the fact that "our master took much pains with us, gave us much practical aid."

Thus he was given the opportunity of "attending large numbers of sick" as a dispensary pupil, years in advance of taking his degree of M.D. in 1841. As a result of this experience he always felt that he had derived "real benefit from a full course of attendance at the Edinburgh Infirmary."

The newly qualified young doctor spent the winter of 1841-42 in Paris, where not only did he work in many of the hospitals of that great city, but he also attended classes of the École de Médecine.

On his return to Scotland, he was appointed assistant to his former teacher, Professor, later Sir, James Y. Simpson, the latter himself then at the start of his own brilliant career, for it was in 1846 that he first became interested in the uses of ether and chloroform.

After a busy, interesting and productive year as Simpson's assistant, the young doctor Keith again took off on his travels. Over the course of the next few years, he travelled widely. He spent a season in Rome, where he had initially intended to practice for a time, but decided against this due to "the prevalence of homeopathic ideas", which he felt he could not adopt.

He then journeyed to the East, where he did practice, mostly in Syria and Palestine. Again he was kept fully occupied in his practice of medicine and over time, his patients, introduced by his dragoman or interpreter, included fabulously wealthy Arab sheiks and Turkish pashas; while at the other end of the scale, he ministered to the dirt-poor in their wretched hovels, tents and disease-ridden villages.

In 1845, Professor Simpson invited the young and already highly experienced Doctor Keith to join him as colleague, and he continued in this appointment until 1850. It was during his five years as colleague to the great man that chloroform was introduced. As Dr. Keith later observed "I was often asked to try the drug as manufactured by different chemists, and also to try instruments which were at first considered necessary in using it." During this time, many of these experiments took place at the home of Professor Simpson. In addition, Dr. Keith, who was then prone to headaches and sleeplessness, took the drug two or three times a day for a considerable period and not only to relieve his own symptoms but also by way of further experiment "to see if any evil results would follow."

A Fellow of the Edinburgh College of Physicians since 1845, and generally thought to be a singularly attractive personality, George Keith, on leaving his appointment with Simpson, then went off to practice in Edinburgh until 1880.

When once in general practice on his own account, he gradually formulated his own ideas, devoting himself, his energies and his very considerable talents to popularising the theory and practice of 'the simple life'.

And what exactly did such a theory entail? Dr. Keith had strong convictions regarding not only the prevalence but the very real dangers inherent in over-eating and in the abuse of alcohol. A firm believer that diet had an active and positive part to play not only in the maintenance of day-to-day health, but also in the actual treatment of everything from rheumatic fever to cancer, this remarkable pioneer doctor practised exactly what he preached.

He propounded his ideas that a simple diet is best for health, and this theory he would explain in the greatest detail to anyone else who stood still long enough to listen to him!

And what exactly were the basic ingredients of 'a simple diet'? To find this out, we can best examine the sum total of the good doctor's own daily food intake.

Two or three slices of brown bread, tea without sugar, a small tumbler of milk, vegetable soup made with no meat stock, about three ounces of fish, a potato and other vegetables fresh from the garden, and finally a helping of fresh, baked or stewed fruit. Yes, it all sounds very familiar to us, close on a hundred years later, when virtually every magazine carries at least one simple diet for 'healthy' eating.

In addition to a strict diet, Dr. Keith also held firmly to his belief that four things were essential in the treatment of almost any illness ...... rest to the stomach by cutting out food at the onset of the illness: rest to the body by sending the invalid to the warmth and comfort of bed: fresh air: and, finally, supplies of hot water for the patient to drink.

Following this régime, both as to diet and to treatment of any of his own illnesses, when he was 78 years of age, Dr. Keith wrote;

'On this diet I enjoy the best of health and for my age, am up to a fair amount of exercise, walking three to six miles daily in good, sometimes in bad, weather, and usually part of this is up a steep road with a rise of 250 feet.'

For fully forty years, he kept strictly to the rule that if he at any time felt unwell, he at once stopped all food intake and drank nothing but large draughts of hot water. If this 'treatment' in itself was not sufficient, he would then advocate for himself bed-rest until such time as good health had been fully restored.

As well as being known as 'The Starving Doctor of Edinburgh', George Keith was also sometimes referred to as 'The Apostle of Hot Water.' This additional nickname came about after another doctor, writing in the Edinburgh Medical Journal of Keith's insistence that his patients drink lots of water, referred to this pioneer of a simple, meat-free diet, as 'The Apostle of Hot Water.'

The Apostle of Hot Water

And in later life did George Keith ever allow himself any dietary 'treats' or other concessions to advancing old age? Well, he did admit to having 'one confession to make.' Then fast approaching eighty years of age, he allowed himself the luxury of 'when at home, I do not rise till I have had breakfast and read the newspaper.' He went on in one of his books to recommend this particular habit to others of a similar age, pointing out that those octogenarians who had already tried such a régime, admitted to feeling 'stronger for the rest of the day.'

As to breakfast, George Keith said 'I enjoy breakfast just as much as my other meals, though I never feel what can be called hunger, and have not done so for many years'. He further pointed out that in his view if anyone could omit a meal at any time without discomfort, then that was undoubtedly 'the best proof of perfect digestion.'

Throughout his life, this pioneering and far-seeing doctor was often reviled for his strongly-held and then extremely unorthodox views and theories. That being so, he must have taken comfort from the Press Reviews of his companion volume *Plea For A Simpler Life.*

The treatise is a powerful argument against the abuse of food and stimulants, both in health and sickness. *(St. James's Budget.)*

This is a charming little book. There is much sound common sense and a great deal of solid truth in what he says, and his little book deserves to be widely read. *(Manchester Guardian.)*

Most of us, I suppose, want to live as long as we can, and to make our lives as comfortable as possible. Various counsellors in all ages have given advice with a view to the attainment of these desirable ideals, but I am not sure that any one of them hits the nail on the head with a finer precision than is achieved by Dr. George S. Keith, whose Plea For a Simpler Life is of sturdy common sense all compact. *(The New Age)*

His opinions may be read with advantage. *(The Times)*

Whatever discussion may arise over this book between the author and his fellow medical men, the fact will not be altered that there is much in it to be carefully considered by most of us. *(The Scotsman)*

As one who has 'carefully considered' *Plea For a Simpler Life* and also *Fads of an Old Physician*, albeit close to a century later, I, too, would add my praise of Dr. George Keith and his theories. In my own drug-free, healthy-eating approach to severe osteo-arthritis, I, too, feel that I owe a debt of gratitude to the good doctor.

It is interesting also to note that many of those who took to the simpler life under Dr. Keith's direction attained a great age. And what of 'The Starving Doctor' himself? He did not retire until in his eighties, and even then, lived a full life with his writing, walking, exercising, foreign travel and voluminous correspondence with friends worldwide until his 91st year, when he died, and was buried at Currie, Midlothian. Although he himself is now a part of history, his ideas live on. Yes! Truly Dr. George S. Keith was one of Scotland's most important innovators.

CONCLUSION

And finally...

It is hoped that the contents of this book will have intrigued, entertained and in some cases, perhaps even mildly amused the reader. If nothing else, these case-histories and events will have served to underline the fact, the indisputable fact, that there is nothing new, even in this so-called 'enlightened' age. It has all been done before and by Scottish visionaries, all of them pioneers in their particular field.

It is also hoped that the reading of such a diversity of life-styles will even have inspired some retired or unemployed people to 'have a go' at an alternative life-style and/or a new career. One thing is sure, it is never too late to embark on such an undertaking - as take the case of the somewhat elderly Mary Ogilvie.

This remarkable lady was ninety-three years of age when she decided to start on her literary career. But what was she to write about? Even she, unskilled in the ways of writers, knew that as a 'late developer', she would need an extra-special topic with which to entice a publisher, not to mention the discriminating reading public.

Obviously someone must have given her that time-honoured piece of advice to all aspiring writers - "Write about what you know." Despite the fact that never throughout her life had she kept a diary or a journal of any kind, as with many elderly people, her distant memory was excellent. This meant that she had total recall of the years of her girlhood and could picture in precise detail every nuance, every event, and indeed every outfit she had worn. So, if there was one thing she knew about, it was most definitely her childhood. The idea once conceived, she at once got to work on her proposed book.

'A SCOTTISH CHILDHOOD - AND WHAT HAPPENED AFTER.'

Her fascinating manuscript also featured a vivid account of her voyage around the world in those far-off years when, not only was it virtually unheard of for a woman to attempt such an undertaking, it was also a very real achievement.

In writing of her great adventure, she dwelt in some detail of a period of time spent in the Peruvian Andes during the year 1877. That distant country might just as well have been on another planet for all that was then known of it to people in Britain and in Europe. That being so, far from the usual stream of rejections as encountered by most aspiring authors, the redoubtable Miss Mary Ogilvie, with little or no difficulty, found a willing publisher.

So it was that shortly after her **ninety-third birthday**, her remarkable book, with even the very title still unchanged by her doting publisher, became a reality. And when 'A SCOTTISH CHILDHOOD - AND WHAT HAPPENED AFTER' was published, hit the news-stands and sold well to an intrigued and highly appreciative audience, Mary Ogilvie became something of a celebrity.

No, it is never too late to start on a new project, of whatever variety appeals to each individual person. For surely that is the entire point? We *are* all individuals and no two lives, despite how many similarities there may be, can ever be the same.

As was pointed out in the introduction, it is indeed intriguing as to the vagaries of Fate, and as to what we each of us make of the skills, temperaments and untapped resources with which we daily face life.

'Doing one's own thing' was thought to be an extremely modern concept of the latter half of the 20th Century - perhaps we are none of us quite so innovative as we thought?